ALSO BY HORTON FOOTE

MEMOIR

Farewell

PLAYS AND SCREENPLAYS

The Orphans' Home Cycle
Horton Foote Collected Works Volume III
Horton Foote Collected Plays Volume II
Four New Plays
Selected One-Act Plays of Horton Foote
Three Screenplays by Horton Foote
Four Plays from the Orphans' Home Cycle
Three Plays from the Orphans' Home Cycle
Two Plays from the Orphans' Home Cycle

A MEMOIR

Horton Foote

SCRIBNER

NEW YORK   LONDON   TORONTO   SYDNEY   SINGAPORE

SCRIBNER
1230 Avenue of the Americas
New York, NY 10020

For information regarding special discounts for bulk purchases, please contact
Simon & Schuster Special Sales at 1-800-456-6798 or
business@simonandschuster.com

Design by Colin Joh
Set in Garamond

Manufactured in the United States of America

1 3 5 7 9 10 8 6 4 2

The Library of Congress has catalogued the Scribner edition as follows:
Foote, Horton
Beginnings: a memoir/Horton Foote
p.   cm.
1. Foote, Horton. 2. Dramatists, American—20th century—Biography.
3. Screenwriters—United States—Biography. I. Title.
PS3511.O344 Z466 2001   812'54—dc21   [B]   2001047088
ISBN 0-7432-1115-4
0-7432-1116-2 (Pbk)

In memory of my wife, Lillian Vallish Foote

things have ends and beginnings. . . .
—Ezra Pound
Canto LXXVI

PART I

Pasadena

CHAPTER 1

By the time our bus was reaching the outskirts of Los Angeles there were very few of the original Dallas passengers left. James Hall's sister was still here but somewhere back in New Mexico she had gotten bored with me and changed seats and now I could hear her talking away with a man who had come aboard in Phoenix. I was sitting next to a lady from Tucson now. She was worried to death about the Depression. She and her husband had lost everything because of it, and she wanted to know if I thought Roosevelt was doing enough. I said I had great faith in Roosevelt. She asked me why, but I couldn't answer that except to say that my father had and he knew a lot about politics. She sighed and looked out the window and then I began to think of Pasadena and tried to imagine what the playhouse might look like.

"Excuse me," the lady said. "What does your father do?"

"He has a men's clothing store and he manages my grandmother's cotton farms."

"Are you an only child?" she wanted to know. Why on earth, I couldn't imagine.

"No, ma'am, I have two brothers."

"Older or younger?"

"Younger."

"I have no children." She sighed when she said that.

"Yes, ma'am."

"Your parents are blessed to have three children. My husband and I wanted children, but the Lord saw it another way. Bless be the name of the Lord. Where are you going, young man?"

"Pasadena."

"Why?"

"Because I want to be an actor."

There was a pause while she thought that over.

"I would think," she said, "you would go to Hollywood for that, if you want to be in the movies."

"Yes, ma'am, but I don't want to be in the movies. I want to go on the stage and there is a school in Pasadena that will teach you about acting."

"About acting?" she asked and she seemed genuinely puzzled.

"Yes, ma'am."

There was a pause again as she thought that over. Then she sighed and looked at me and said, "What does it cost to learn something like that?"

"Five hundred dollars for the first year and two hundred and fifty dollars for the second year."

"My God," she said, sighing. "That's expensive."

"I know it is," I said.

"Do they guarantee you a job when you finish your schooling?"

"No, ma'am."

"Mercy," she said, sighing again. "How much did you say?"

"Five hundred dollars the first year and two hundred and fifty dollars the second."

"Let's see," she said. "What does that come to?"

"Seven hundred and fifty dollars," I said. A figure my father had drummed into my head.

"Mercy," she said, sighing. "Your people must be rich."

"No, ma'am," I said. "Not my daddy anyway. I have a grandmother that's pretty well off I'm told."

"Is she paying for it?"

"No, ma'am, my daddy is."

She sighed again then and closed her eyes. I looked out the window of the bus, but I couldn't see much except houses that looked like houses anywhere, or at least like houses I could see anytime in Texas.

The lady opened her eyes then and looked up at me, and said, "Seven hundred and fifty dollars is a fortune to me. A fortune."

"Yes, ma'am," I said, and I wished she would get off the subject. I felt guilty enough about my daddy spending the money without her going on about it.

"We lost our home," the lady said, "Our car. My God, this Depression is a terrible thing. Terrible."

"Yes, ma'am," I said. "I know it is," and I knew in my heart it certainly must be, and I knew I should be concerned about it, and worry about it like my daddy and his friends at his store, but all I could think about was getting to Pasadena and starting school. My mother had told me that my Great Aunt Mag and her husband, Uncle Walt, were going to meet me at the Los Angeles bus station, and then I began to worry about what I would do if for some reason they couldn't get there. How would I get to Pasadena? Now stop worrying about that, I said to myself. My mother says they are very dependable and they're sure to be there. Before I had a chance to worry any further the lady next to me took two snapshots from her purse and held them up for me to see.

"This is the picture of the house we lost to the bank," she said. "And this is the car. I'm going to Los Angeles to stay with my people until my husband can get on his feet again. We have no children, thank God. I don't know what we'd do if we had children to feed and clothe. I hope to heavens your father is right and Roosevelt does know what he's doing. Why does it take so long? This is September, September nineteen hundred and thirty-four. He's had almost two years. How long is it going to take?"

I looked out the window, but it was getting dark now and I couldn't see much except for lights coming from the houses we were passing.

The lady next to me called out to the lady across the aisle. "This boy," she said pointing to me, "is going to acting school. It's costing seven hundred and fifty dollars. Isn't that right, son?"

"Yes, ma'am," I said closing my eyes, hoping she would leave me alone, when the bus driver called out: "We're coming into Los Angeles."

I tried to look out the window again but it was pitch black outside now and I couldn't see anything but the lights of houses and cars. Then I could see streetlights and buildings and more cars and people on the sidewalks and the lady across the aisle said, "We're almost at the terminal now."

We rode on for another five or ten minutes and the bus pulled into the terminal, which was all lit up and seemed much larger than the Houston or Dallas bus terminals. The bus driver stopped the bus and called out, "Los Angeles!" and everyone began to get up from their seats. The lady next to me patted me on the arm as we started down the aisle and said, "Good luck to you, son," and I thanked her. I got off the bus and followed the people into the terminal. I saw Aunt Mag and Uncle Walt right away and they saw me. Aunt Mag hugged me and kissed me and Uncle Walt shook my hand as he said, "Welcome to California."

Aunt Mag was my grandmother's next-to-youngest sister. She immediately began asking question after question about our family in Texas. She idolized my grandmother and constantly interrupted my answers with descriptions of her kindness. She continued the questioning while we went to pick up my suitcase, which Uncle Walt insisted on carrying. Finally she stopped long enough to ask if I was hungry. I said I was, and she asked if I would mind eating in a cafeteria. I said I didn't know as I never had. I was about to say that wherever they wanted to eat would be fine with me, but before I could she began to explain why she preferred this cafeteria. Not because it was cheaper than a restaurant, but because the food was the best she knew of in Los Angeles, and without looking at Uncle Walt she asked if he agreed. He nodded his head that he did, and I said that all I knew about cafeterias was that my Aunt Laura and Erin May went to one in Houston and got ptomaine poisoning from eating some butterscotch pie. "Well, that was Houston," Aunt Mag said. "Nothing like that could happen in Los Angeles, could it, Walt?"

When we got to the cafeteria they instructed me to pick up a tray, napkin, silverware and showed me where to stand in line. I had not seen so much food on display before in my life and I had great difficulty making a decision about what to eat. I hadn't been able to sleep much on the bus, but I was so exhilarated about finally being in California that I didn't feel tired. The cafeteria seemed very glamorous, lit up as it was, and decorated in what seemed to me a very modern fashion. During dinner she said they would show me some of the sights if I was interested. I said I was. After we finished eating we got in their car and Uncle Walt drove us around Los Angeles. We passed some palm trees and Aunt Mag said, "I guess you know what they are?"

"Yes, ma'am," I said. "Palm trees." They seemed much larger than the palm trees I'd seen in Houston and Galveston. I asked my father once why we didn't have any in Wharton, and he said our soil was the wrong kind for palm trees. "Aunt Mag," I asked. "Do the palm trees have coconuts?"

"No," she said. "They don't. Why is that, Walt?"

"Why is what?" he asked.

"Why don't our palm trees have coconuts?"

"I don't know," he said. "I've never heard."

"Well, you should ask somebody," she said.

"I will," he said. "One day."

"That's your Uncle Walt, for you," she said. "No curiosity about anything."

My mother and grandmother had assured me Aunt Mag and Uncle Walt would have me stay in their Los Angeles apartment for an evening. Then they would drive me over to the YMCA in Pasadena where I would stay until the school office assigned me to a boardinghouse. After an hour or so of riding I was beginning to feel tired and I was about to ask if we could go to their apartment so I could get to bed, when Aunt Mag said, "Walt, we'd better take him out to Pasadena, so he can get settled." I wanted to say, Oh no, ma'am, I'm supposed to stay with you and Uncle Walt tonight, but I felt shy and couldn't bring myself to say it.

Pasadena was quite a drive from Los Angeles. Aunt Mag pointed out that we were passing through orange groves to get there, and it was too bad it was so dark out because they were quite beautiful.

When we finally got to the YMCA, I was so tired I could hardly keep my eyes open and Aunt Mag kept repeating over and over, "Look Walt, it's a handsome building. I wouldn't mind staying there myself—Look Walt, look Horton, isn't it handsome?" I agreed I thought it was and then she said, "Walt, help him with his suitcase and be sure they have a room for him." "All right, Mag," Uncle Walt said, some of the few words he had spoken during the whole evening.

He got my suitcase out of the back of the car and I kissed Aunt Mag good-bye and I said I would call her and give her my telephone number when I knew where I would be living.

"All right, honey," she said. "We want you to spend Thanksgiving with us in Vista with our children."

I knew all their children lived in Vista, where Aunt Mag and Uncle Walt had once lived and I started to say my mother said she felt sure you would have me for Thanksgiving, but I didn't. I followed Uncle Walt into the YMCA. After Uncle Walt heard they had a room available for me he said he'd better be off as it was late and they had a long ride back to Los Angeles.

My room was small, but clean, and I was so tired I fell on the bed and went to sleep with my clothes on.

I woke up early the next morning and decided not to unpack

my suitcase, since I would soon be moving to my permanent home. I went to the lobby and asked the clerk where I could get breakfast. He directed me to a drugstore a block and a half away.

The drugstore breakfast—eggs, bacon, coffee, and orange juice—cost twenty-five cents, and I was about to ask for a second cup of coffee, when I thought I had better not because they might charge me for it and I knew I had to be careful with my money.

I paid my check and asked the clerk where the Pasadena Playhouse was, and he said he didn't know as he had never heard of it, but a lady buying perfume said she knew. I asked if it was in walking distance. She said yes and told me how to get there.

I found the street it was on and in the distance I could hear church bells ringing from every direction. Pasadena, as I later found out, was a city of churches. I saw a building up ahead with a patio in front. There were two small shops and a small restaurant all on one side of the patio, all closed on a Sunday morning. I stopped to look inside the patio and I saw on the side of the building a closed ticket booth, and I called out to a man walking by. I asked if this was the Pasadena Playhouse and he said yes. I looked at my watch and saw it was almost noon and I thought about what I was going to do until the next morning when the school opened. I thought then of my mother and father and realized when it was noon here it was two o'clock in Texas. I knew they had probably done this Sunday what they did every Sunday. Mother had cooked a Sunday breakfast, grits certainly, ham or bacon and eggs, and biscuits, fig preserves, or maybe sausage instead of bacon or ham, and after breakfast my father would sit in the living room and read the Sunday paper, and Mother would go to the Methodist church with my brothers. I couldn't remember whether it was her Sunday to play the organ or whether it was my cousin Daisy Armstrong's. Then I suddenly thought of Miss Mina Barclay, who had also shared the organ playing until she committed suicide, hanging herself in her bedroom. I thought of my father's store and I wondered how much business he had done the day before. Saturday was always the day he made money if he was to make any money. I knew the cotton crop had looked promising if it didn't suddenly start raining and they could get it picked and to the gin. I looked up at the California sky to see that the sun was shining and I wondered if it was shining at home. I hoped so, because the last thing the cotton needed this time of the year was rain. I thought of my father locking up the store at night and wondered, since it was Saturday, how late he had stayed open and whether he had gone to Ray's or the Manhattan Restaurant for fried oysters, like he did when I worked with him. I thought of walking home with him down the dirt road after our meal at the restaurant and being greeted by my mother as we came into the house, and my father telling her how his business had been. I thought of my bedroom then and my bed, and I realized my brother was sleeping in my bed now and that gave me a funny feeling. I looked up at the street sign and it said Colorado Boulevard, and I thought of the river at home, the Colorado. I looked up and down Colorado Boulevard, and I knew I was where I wanted to be, or thought I wanted to be, in Pasadena, California.

Or did I? I really wanted to go to New York City, but I came here because it was best, my father said, for a boy of seventeen to be in a smaller city. Colorado Boulevard was wide, but there was little traffic on this Sunday morning, and I thought of Aunt Mag and Uncle Walt in Los Angeles and I wondered what they were doing and I wished now I had said I was supposed to spend the night. Even with hardly any people around I knew I was in a city. All the buildings up and down the street told me so. Not a town like Wharton. I was all alone and didn't know where to go or what to do. I thought, I'll go back to my room at the YMCA, and maybe write a letter to my mother and father. What would I tell them, that Aunt Mag and Uncle Walt didn't ask me to spend the night and left me alone with nothing to do? No, I couldn't write that, because it would worry them. I'd just say I arrived safe and sound, loved Pasadena, had a look at the outside of the playhouse, and I was very excited and couldn't wait until I met my teachers on Monday and saw where I was to live.

But where were the flowers? There were a few palm trees every now and again, but no flowers. I had seen pictures of Pasadena in the news reels at the times of the Rose Bowl parades, and flowers, particularly roses, seemed to be everywhere you looked. My grandmother had been to California and she said to her dying day she would never get over the flowers. Bougainvillaea was her favorite, she said. She tried growing it at home, but a cold spell killed it. Her Confederate jasmine lasted through all the cold spells, but not the bougainvillaea.

I thought about New York City then and I wondered what I would be doing there if my parents had allowed me to go. My cousin Nannie said it was the most exciting place she'd ever been in, even more fun than New Orleans and she did love New Orleans. She said the only thing she didn't like about it was the subways. She was afraid to ride them, but New Yorkers rode them all the time. I wondered when I finally got there if I'd be afraid of them.

I walked up and down Colorado Boulevard for an hour or more looking in the shop windows. I saw a movie house. I forget now what picture was playing, but it was nothing I wanted to see. Even if it had been, I don't think I would have spent money on a ticket. I passed a cafeteria like the one my aunt and uncle had taken me to the night before, only smaller. I tried to see without going inside how much things cost, but I didn't see any signs, so I decided not to go in, and turned back toward the YMCA. I saw a small restaurant, no tables, just a counter and stools. I went in and they had the prices of the food over the counter. I saw they had a hamburger for ten cents, and I ordered one and also a Coke. It was two o'clock by then and four o'clock in Wharton. Church was over and our cook had fried the chicken for Sunday dinner. I wanted to find a telephone and call them up but I knew I shouldn't, because my mother and father were making a real sacrifice sending me to dramatic school and we had to all be very careful how we spent our money. So I went back to the YMCA. The lobby was empty and no one around except the desk clerk, who was reading a paper. I thought, It wouldn't break me to buy a paper and that will give me something to do.

"Excuse me, do you know where I can buy a Sunday paper?" I said as I went up to the clerk.

"No," he said. "Not really, but I'm through with this, you can have it if you want it."

"Thank you," I said. "How much is it?"

"No," he said. "I'm giving it to you."

"Thank you," I said.

So I took the paper and thanked him again and started for my room.

"We have a swimming pool here, you know," he called after me. "You can go for a swim if you want to."

"Thank you," I said. "But I didn't bring a bathing suit."

"You don't need a bathing suit here," he said. "Only men use the pool, everyone swims naked."

"Thank you," I said. "I'll think about it."

I was too embarrassed to say I couldn't swim, so I just went up to my room and read the paper and wrote a letter to my mother and father. I was suddenly so tired I fell across the bed and went to sleep. When I woke up it was almost ten o'clock, twelve o'clock at home, I thought. My folks were all in bed asleep, and I thought, I'll never get to sleep now after this long nap, but before long I was sleepy again and I undressed and put on my pajamas and was soon back to sleep.

CHAPTER 2

Pasadena Playhouse

I was up early the next morning, went to the YMCA office, paid my bill, took my suitcase, and began my walk to the playhouse. It was only seven thirty by then and I knew the school office didn't open until nine, so I went to the drugstore where I had eaten the morning before and spent another twenty-five cents for breakfast. I lingered over my coffee as long as I could, but the drugstore was filling up with customers and I decided I'd better finish my coffee and let someone have my seat at the counter. I paid my bill and walked slowly down the street toward the playhouse.

It was eight thirty when I got there. The restaurant and the stores still weren't open. The patio was empty except for a blond young man in a rumpled dark suit. He was smoking a cigarette and when he saw me with my suitcase he came over.

"Are you going to school here?" he asked.

"Yes."

"I am, too. My name is Forsht. John Forsht."

"Hi. I'm Horton Foote."

"Where are you from?"

"Texas."

"I'm from Pennsylvania. Did you just get in?"

"No. I came in Saturday night. I've been staying at the YMCA."

"I just got here. I found somebody at the Los Angeles bus station that was coming to Pasadena and they gave me a ride. You had breakfast?"

"Yes. You?"

"No. I had coffee. I haven't eaten for two days."

"Why?"

"It's a long sad story." He threw his cigarette away. "Do you smoke?"

"Yes."

"That was my last cigarette. Do you have any on you?"

"Yes."

"Would you give me one?"

"Sure." I took out my package of cigarettes and handed it to him. "Take a couple."

"Thanks." He did so. He lit the cigarette and shook his head dolefully. "You wouldn't believe what happened to me. I had to change buses in Denver, and had a two-hour wait for the bus to Los Angeles and this man came over to me, a nice-looking man, and he said, 'Are you from the East,' and I said I was, and he said he could tell, he can always tell an easterner and then he said he hoped to get East one day and had I ever been to New York City and I said no, but I had gone to school in Philadelphia and he said, 'Where,' and I said, 'Gerard College.' He said he's never heard of it and I said it was endowed by a man named Gerard for boys whose fathers were dead, and he said, 'An orphanage,' and I said no, it wasn't that, as most of us there still had mothers and he looked up at the clock in the station then and he said, 'Oh, boy, I almost missed my bus,' and he went running away. Minutes later I went to get a Coke and a sandwich and I reached for my wallet to take out a dollar bill, and it was gone. That man had stolen it."

"I'm sorry."

"Can you believe it?"

"My daddy told me to watch out for pickpockets. What will you do?"

"Well, I'm on scholarship here and my room and board was paid in advance and I'll be all right once I get in my boarding-house. Then my brother will send me a little money so I can start eating lunches again. You couldn't spare a quarter now, could you? I'll pay you back in a week as soon as my brother can get some money to me."

"Sure."

"Thanks."

I gave him a quarter and he started off as other young people began to arrive.

At nine o'clock a man came down the patio steps and said the school office was across the street. He told us to follow him and we did as he crossed the street to the house that looked like a house and not like a school office at all. I tried, without being noticed, to size up my fellow students walking with me across the street. There were twelve girls and seven boys. None of them looked any different than my schoolmates back in Wharton, except for one very beautiful girl, a platinum blond, dressed very well. Another I noticed was a middle-aged woman and when I heard her ask a question I realized she had an accent. What kind I didn't know. Some of the prospective students seemed to know each other, and one girl, very stout, and dressed very flamboyantly, had a southern accent and kept telling everybody she was from Fort Worth, Texas, and that her name was Jody Schwartzberg. There were only two more people with suitcases and I found out later that most of the students were from the Los Angeles area and their parents had driven them over the night before as they had already been told where they were going to live.

Inside the house, just off the front hall, was the office and a lady in her early thirties, very regal looking, dressed in white, like she was about to play tennis. The man who had guided us over pointed to the regal lady and said, "This is Miss Eugenia Ong." Miss Ong smiled and said in a very cultured accent, "Welcome. I'm also your speech teacher."

After signing registration forms I was given the address of my boardinghouse on Oakland Avenue and was told I would now have the rest of the day to get settled in my new home and to report for classes at nine the next morning.

My boardinghouse, within walking distance of the school, was a two-story yellow frame house on a small yard with no flowers or shrubs. The owner of the boardinghouse, a plump, cheerful, nervous lady in her early fifties, said all her boarders called her "Boss," which I did from then on with such regularity that I have forgotten her real name, which I'm sure was told me that first day. There was another student from the playhouse, she said, going to live at the boardinghouse, Charles Robinson from Hawaii, but he wasn't due until late afternoon. There were two other boarders, elderly men, who had lived here a number of years, I was told. Linens were changed once a week and I was responsible to make my own bed each day, which I had never done in Wharton, and which I had only done haphazardly for the past few days.

My room was on the second floor. The walls were plaster and painted a very pale green. There were no pictures on the walls. A bed, a table, a straight chair, and a larger armchair were the only furnishings in the room. I tried the bed and it was comfortable enough. The Boss, when she brought me to my room, pointed out that Mr. Taylor, the older of the two men, had the room next to mine on the right and Monte (she never told me his last name or if she did I've forgotten it) had the room on the left. Charles Robinson was farther down the hall next to Monte.

I was in the living room that evening promptly at seven and the Boss was there with the two older boarders. They were listening to the radio.

"Come in," she said cheerfully, "and meet Mr. Taylor and Monte. Mr. Taylor is a bookkeeper and Monte is a postman. This is Horton. He's going to be part of our family now."

The two men turned from the radio to look at me. Mr. Taylor was in his late sixties, and had the look of a man that spent his days behind an office desk and never out in the sun. He seemed kind enough and nodded and smiled at me as I went over to shake his hand.

"Welcome," he said.

"Thank you, sir," I said.

Monte's face was a deep tan. Obviously, he spent hours in the sun delivering mail.

"Where you from?" he asked.

"Texas," I said.

Charles Robinson, a thin, handsome boy, arrived then with his suitcase. The Boss went to greet him.

"Well," she said, "here's our friend from Honolulu. This is Charles Robinson."

He looked at me, smiled, and walked over to me extending his hand.

"Hi."

"Hi," I said, "I'm Horton."

"He's from Texas," the Boss said.

Charles then went to the other men and introduced himself.

"You visit now," the Boss said, "or listen to the radio. I'll get our dinner on the table."

I was up early for breakfast the next morning and was about to start off for school when Charles Robinson appeared and begged me to wait while he had his breakfast so we could walk to school together.

John Forsht, the boy I had loaned a quarter to, was there when we arrived, as were a number of other students, all I'm sure as nervous and full of self-doubt as I was, and covering up their nervousness by constant chatter. Jody Schwartzberg, the stout girl from Fort Worth, was talking about her trip to New York City the previous summer and how disappointed she was that the Civic Repertory Theater had closed for the summer and perhaps permanently because of the stock market crash. She said it caused Eva Le Gallienne, "the greatest actress in America if not in all the world," to lose all her wealthy backers. One girl asked who Miss Le Gallienne was and what was the Civic Repertory Theater. Her question was greeted with sarcasm by Jody, who then began a long lecture about the Civic Repertory Theater and Miss Le Gallienne, including all her acting credits.

Our classes were five days a week from nine to five with an hour off for lunch. We took lessons in eurythmics, fencing, speech, history of theater, scene design, French, and makeup. We had two hours of rehearsals, in which the three directors of the plays given on the main stage of the playhouse took turns directing us in plays to be performed, without scenery and only once, for our fellow students. The first two of these plays were a Roman comedy, the title of which I have mercifully forgotten, and *Shakuntula,* a classic East Indian play. I had never heard of either of them, nor had any of the other students. Our directors were to be Lenore Shanewise and Thomas Brown Henry.

After a few days of classes, some of the faces and names came into focus for me, so when someone spoke of Peter Engel, for instance, I could immediately pick him out among the other students. Peter, tall and gangly, wearing glasses, with ruddy cheeks, spoke English as if it were not his native language. Early on he began paying attention to Peggy Carter, tiny, petite, and always unfailingly cheerful. She seemed even more petite next to him. We soon accepted them as a couple.

The name Skouras meant nothing to me, but I soon learned that to Californians, with any knowledge of motion picture studio hierarchy, it was a name to be in awe of, and I soon began to realize that Margi, with lovely brown eyes and golden curls, was treated with great deference by the other students because she was the daughter of a Skouras. Not *the* Skouras, but the daughter of his brother, a lesser Skouras, powerful enough in his own way. I asked Charles Robinson who the Skourases were and why everyone was so in awe of them as we walked to our boardinghouse together.

"Come with me," he said and started walking in the direction of Colorado Boulevard.

"Where are we going?" He didn't answer my question but kept going until we reached Colorado and when we got there he stopped and pointed to the movie house.

"What does the sign on that movie house say?"

"Skouras," I answered. I had never noticed it before.

"They own a chain of theaters all over Los Angeles and her uncle is head of Fox Studio."

"Well, then," I said. "Margi has nothing to worry about if she wants to act in pictures. She'll get jobs for sure."

"I don't know," Charles said. "I hear her family are very strict, very religious, and don't think much of actresses, and not too happy she wants to be one."

John Pelletti, who had become friendly with John Forsht and me, had his eye on Margi Skouras, but had already found out that she was under strict supervision, not allowed to date. She could only marry someone chosen by her father. How he knew this I don't know. The Skourases were Greek Catholics, a denomination I had never heard of before. It had to be explained to me the differences between Greek Catholics and Roman Catholics. Mary Virginia Palmer, from Phoenix, Arizona, I soon learned was a devout Roman Catholic, and went to Mass regularly. John Pelletti, warm-hearted and likeable, had also been raised a Roman Catholic, he told John Forsht and me, but never went to Mass and thought it all of no importance. Mary Virginia, with a very prominent nose, looked more Greek to me than Margi Skouras.

The two other Marys in our group, Mary Todd and Mary Green, though strangers before starting school, soon became friends. Mary Green was an enthusiast of Ethel Barrymore, the renowned stage star, and the other Mary was devoted to movie actress Ruth Chatterton. Mary Green was older than most of us and had a patrician manner about her walk and speech. Mary Todd, nearsighted and wearing glasses, was friendly, outgoing, and a great mimic.

I was early on, and continued to be my first year at the playhouse, enamored of Charlotte Sturges. She looked like a sturdy, less ethereal Katharine Hepburn and spoke with the clipped speech of Hepburn. She was interested in modern dance and her ambition was to go to Germany and study with Mary Wigman, the great modern dancer. I knew little of modern dance and nothing of Mary Wigman before I met Charlotte, but she wanted to talk of nothing else, and so I soon learned a great deal about both. Charlotte had brought her drum with her to school and had already began choreographing solo dances to her drum accompaniment.

The day arrived that the casts of the plays were to be announced. I was so excited that I wasn't able to sleep the night before. I kept fantasizing about the kind of play it would be, and what part I would be given. At home Eppie Murphree had always given me the leads and I knew I couldn't expect that to happen here in Pasadena with so many students wanting parts, but I hoped at least I would be given an interesting one, in an interesting play.

John Forsht, John Pelletti, Peter Engel, and I were to be in the Roman comedy, along with Peggy, Peter Engel's girlfriend, and Jody Schwartzberg. I forget now who else was in it, nor do I remember much else about it. The play was a miserable experience for me. My sides made no sense to me, and when Tom Brown Henry, our director, announced he was going to read the play to us, I thought, Now I'll understand what's going on, but I didn't. The other students began to laugh at certain lines, but I thought they were forcing their laughter to get in good with the director and later John Forsht and John Pelletti agreed with me. Tom Brown Henry, a talented but sarcastic man, felt the best method of helping you grow as an actor was to make insulting but witty remarks about your lack of talent and experience. He had one poor girl, Ruth Lewis, paralyzed with fear. She moved with such tension, her face flushed beet red, that I thought she was going to have a stroke.

"Loosen up," he called out to her, "loosen up, for God's sakes, you're not playing a dummy in a department store window. Loosen up. Try again."

She tried again and again and each time she got even tenser.

"Is that what you call loosening up?" he barked.

She began to cry then and he stopped rehearsals until, he said, she calmed down. The lady with the accent I had observed the first day had been watching rehearsals. She went to the girl and put her arms around her comforting her.

"You know who that is?" Jody Schwartzberg whispered to me.

"No," I whispered back.

"That's Barbara Vajda. She's married to Ernest Vajda."

"Who is Ernest Vajda?"

"He's a famous Hungarian playwright. He's under contract to Metro Goldwyn Mayer. They're rich. She is driven to school every day by her chauffeur in her limousine. She's not here to study acting, but wants to direct."

After Ruth Lewis had calmed down, Tom Brown Henry asked us all to come near him in front of the room.

"Now," he began as we were seating ourselves. "Now, I have to say this to you. The theater is a tough place. To survive you have to be tough. Now I'm not going to help you by flattering you and telling you how good you are. You are here to learn, I believe. You won't learn by my flattering you, but by my telling you what you have to do to survive in this lousy business. Now Gilmor Brown, who as you know is the artistic director of the playhouse, will be along one day and give you inspirational talks about how the theater is a temple and you must dedicate yourself unselfishly to it, and that's what he has done and that's worked for him, but I tell you you'll get kicked out of the temple if you don't know how to walk across the stage without looking like an automaton and talking so low you can't be heard. Now let's get back to rehearsal."

The next day he kept stopping me after each one of my speeches.

"Boy," he would bark.

"Yessir," I said.

"Where are you from?"

"Texas," I said.

"Well, is that how they talk in Texas?" he sneered.

"I don't know, sir. I guess so."

"Well, I'm not from Texas and I can't understand a word you are saying."

"Yessir."

He kept after me day after day.

"I can't understand you, son," he'd yell.

"I'm not loud enough?" I would finally ask.

"No. You're loud enough. But you'll never get anywhere with that accent."

"Yessir."

"Say the line again."

"Yessir."

I tried again and again, my heart sinking. I wanted to vanish, to die, to disappear, to be anywhere but in Pasadena in rehearsal. Why did I even think about being an actor. I was afraid if he stopped me again and made fun of my accent (he was by now imitating me by sounding like Amos 'n' Andy), I'd cry like poor Ruth Lewis.

When rehearsals were over John Forsht and John Pelletti said not to pay any attention to him as my accent wasn't nearly as bad as Jody Schwartzberg's and he said nothing about hers. I thanked them for their support, but I was so upset I could hardly eat my dinner and it didn't help that Charles Robinson, who was in *Shakuntula,* babbled on and on about how inspiring the play was and how wonderful the director, Miss Shanewise, was and how brilliant Ralph Clanton, who was playing the lead, was and everybody in the cast agreed he was going to be a major actor one day.

Three days later, after speech class, Miss Ong asked me to wait after the others had gone and told me she thought I should get special help with my accent and recommended studying privately with her teacher, who was living here in Pasadena. I thanked her and she gave me the lady's name and phone number.

I asked John Forsht the next day what he thought I should do. He said he'd think it over.

John Forsht was three years my senior and had been at Bucknell University in Pennsylvania for two years. A member of the Dramatic Society there, he had played in his last year the role of Hamlet as well as Mercutio in *Romeo and Juliet*. He vowed he would some day play Hamlet again and this time in New York. That was all very impressive to me. I hadn't even read *Hamlet* or *Romeo and Juliet,* but I read them at once. He said Alexander Moissi, the great Reinhardt star, was the greatest Hamlet ever and he hoped one day to go to Germany and see him.

The next day John Forsht and John Pelletti and I were having lunch between classes at the fruit market around the corner from the playhouse. I asked John Forsht if he had thought anymore about my studying privately, and he said he had and thought I should at least talk to the lady.

Miss Blanche Townsend, the speech teacher, was a small woman, who carried herself with almost military precision. We met and discussed the price of lessons. I was very taken by Miss Townsend when we met, and I decided to go without lunch and use that money to pay for two lessons a week. She had me buy a book on phonetics and had me work on the players speech from *Hamlet,* and Mercutio's Queen Mab speech from *Romeo and Juliet*. She gave me exercises she said to strengthen my vowels and consonants, and insisted I write out phonetically every word of every part I worked on. I took everything she said to heart and was faithful in doing all she asked me to do.

Miss Townsend's apartment was quite a walk from my boardinghouse. My lessons were at eight in the morning, and the first lessons consisted of speech and breathing exercises. To begin the breathing exercises I was always asked to stand up as straight as possible and then she would place her hand on my diaphragm, which she said I wasn't using properly.

"Breathe in," she would command. I would breathe in.

"Hold it," she would order next. I would hold it.

"Breathe out," she would say and I would breathe out. This would go on for ten or twenty minutes and then she would ask me to recite Hamlet's speech to the players, and I would begin:

"Speak the speech, I pray you, as I pronounced it to you trippingly on the tongue, but if you mouth it, as many of our players do . . . "

She would give me commands all the while I was reciting.

"Move your diaphragm. Listen to what you're saying, now try it again."

"Trippingly on the tongue" was good for another ten minutes, for she would always stop me after "trippingly," and repeated over and over again the word *trippingly* and then had me repeat it, always adding, "now remember *t* is made with the tip of your tongue on the roof of your mouth, now say *tee* for me."

"Tee," I would say.

"Again."

"Tee."

"Again."

"Tee."

"Splendid. Now say it slowly, deliberately. Trippingly on the tongue. Tee-tee-tee. Understood?"

"Yes, ma'am."

"All right, say it."

"Trippingly on the tongue."

"Trippingly, trippingly, trippingly," she said.

"Trippingly, trippingly, trippingly," I repeated.

"Much better. Much, much better."

I was conscientiously, almost desperately, doing the exercises she gave me and the speeches she asked me to memorize. I didn't know what all this had to do with acting, but was taught by my parents that if you worked hard and applied yourself everything would turn out fine one day. Patience, I counseled myself over and over again, patience. Miss Townsend in turn was patient and kind and always tried to be encouraging. I had been working with her for about two weeks when she said she was going to give me a long poem to learn, and when I had finished that successfully, she would let me work on a scene from *Candida* by George Bernard Shaw. She asked if I knew the play and I said I didn't and she asked me to read it. She said I would do the scene with Miss Lorrimor, who shared the apartment with her. I had seen Miss Lorrimor once from a distance when I first began studying and knew she acted sometimes at the playhouse. I asked what scene would we be working on and she said a scene between Marchbanks and Prossy. She then took a book down from the bookshelf and opened it and handed it to me.

"Here's the poem I would like you to read."

It was Browning's "My Last Duchess." I looked at it for a moment and began to read aloud.

"That's my last duchess painted on the wall . . . "

"No. No," Miss Townsend interrupted. "Don't read it aloud yet, read it all through first for yourself."

I did and when I finished I looked up at her.

"Now begin reading aloud."

And so I began.

"That's my last duchess painted on the wall, looking as if she were alive. I call that piece a wonder, now."

And on and on, lesson after lesson, for three weeks until finally one day she said much to my relief, "I think we can leave the duchess alone for a while now and begin on *Candida*."

The lessons certainly must have worked, because when I went home that summer, I learned later that my brother Tom Brooks was charging his friends ten cents to come over to the house to hear me talk.

CHAPTER 3

Gilmore Brown

My mother wrote me every day, long letters full of news of our family, friends, and the town, and nearly always included the menu they'd had for supper, which was our big meal since my father couldn't get home at noon. There was a crisis of some kind in the family, having to do with my uncles I'm sure, but the specifics were never gone into, resulting in their renting our house and moving in with my Grandmother Brooks. My Grandmother Brooks who hadn't been well, she wrote, was coming to California for Christmas and I would spend it with her in La Jolla, where Aunt Bo, her youngest sister, always took a house for a month during the Christmas season.

Gilmor Brown, the artistic director and founder of the playhouse, as Thomas Brown Henry predicted, met with us from time to time to give us inspiring lectures of how the theater was a holy place, a temple, and we must dedicate our lives to serving it. But he didn't talk much about the New York theater.

He had been a minor actor in a California stock company when he was a young man. I gathered not much was happening for him professionally when he came to Pasadena and on a shoestring started the playhouse. He was the only professional connected with the theater at first and used local amateurs in his plays. Though not a great actor or director, he was a visionary, and he had the ability, in the same way that later Margo Jones in Dallas and Nina Vance in Houston had, to inspire people with his ideas. And by the time I arrived he had, by all accounts, an enviable theater complex. All year long he did interesting and often unusual plays on his main stage, and a few blocks away he had the Play Box, a theater-in-the-round, and I believe the first of its kind in America, where new plays and experimental theater was done.

On the weekends we were encouraged by Gilmor Brown to go to the plays on the main stage at the playhouse. I tried to go both Friday and Saturday nights. I always asked Charlotte Sturges to go with me and she usually accepted. We would go afterward for a soda at an ice-cream parlor on Colorado Boulevard, and talk over what we'd seen, at least for a few minutes. But unless it had been an extraordinary production, Charlotte would soon change the subject and talk about her desire to dance and study with Mary Wigman. She had never seen Wigman dance, but had photographs of her and once brought them along for me to see. She had studied the summer before with a student of Wigman's who had come to Los Angeles from Germany to teach. She had wanted to go to Germany to study instead of coming to the playhouse, but her parents wouldn't allow it, and insisted she come to the playhouse first. She had no desire to be an actress, she said, and thought the eurythmics classes ridiculous, anemic and lacking all dynamics. Once in a while she would do some Wigman movements for me, her body taut and strong, her gestures commanding and assertive. I was very impressed. She despised ballet, too, as being decadent and frivolous. She felt Wigman would supplant all this, according to her, frivolous nonsense. Some of the girls that lived at her house said she was a fanatic and obsessive about her interest in dance. They said they could often hear her beating her drum late at night and moving about her room. But I didn't agree with what they said; I admired her determination and surety of purpose.

Some nights when Charlotte and I would go to the playhouse to see a play we would notice a young woman in her early twenties wearing gray slacks and a matching jacket in the fashion made popular by Marlene Dietrich. She was always standing alone in the shadows and seemed to me very mysterious. I thought she might be a movie star and I asked Charlotte if she was and she said she had no idea and didn't care as she had no interest in movie stars, as she thought Hollywood ridiculous and of no importance. One night I noticed there was a man with her, obviously much older, small in stature, but wiry and strong. He moved with precision and when he talked to her, although I couldn't hear what he said, he seemed agitated. She became more languid, it seemed to me, the more intense he became.

A week later I saw this man walking alone across the patio,

and go into the playhouse. Jody Schwartzberg, who seemed to know everything, was in the patio then and I asked who he was and she said Benjamin Zemach and that he was directing and choreographing a production of Oscar Wilde's *Salome.*

"You know who Benjamin Zemach is, don't you?" she asked me in that haughty way she had of talking.

"No."

"Did you ever hear of the Habimah Theater?"

"No."

"They're a famous Jewish acting company. They started in Moscow and did a production of *The Dybbuk* that was famous all over the world. His brother started the company and Zemach's a member. They are in Israel now."

"Why is he here?"

"I don't know."

Mr. Brown sent word to the students that he would welcome us to the dress rehearsal of *Salome,* and though it was on a school night he urged us to attend as he felt it was something that we should all certainly see.

I asked Charlotte if she would like to go with me and at first she resisted and then Jody Schwartzberg announced she had sneaked into rehearsals and there was a young actor, twenty-five years old, playing Herod named Lee Cobb and she thought anyone interested in acting should see him. Someone then said, "Isn't there dancing in it?" Jody said she had heard so, but there was none while she was watching. The minute she heard the word *dancing,* Charlotte changed her mind and said she would like to go.

I met her in the patio a half hour before the curtain. It was a lovely night as I remember, cool in the way only California nights can be. Jody Schwartzberg was there with her entourage. John Forsht had wanted to come, but couldn't because he was working off his scholarship. Margi Skouras was there with her friend Frances Reid. John Pelletti found out that Margi was going and so he came. Jody was giving lectures about Zemach and the Habimah and Lee Cobb to some of the students. Pelletti was talking to Frances and Margi. Charlotte didn't like Jody, found her loud and coarse, so she moved away from them all and I followed her, although I wanted to hear what Jody was saying. The bell rang for the performance and we went into the theater. There were ladders still around the auditorium and light fixtures and jells in the aisles and on some of the seats. The seats were not reserved for the dress rehearsal and Charlotte led me as far away from Jody and her crowd as she could. We heard Gilmor Brown call from the balcony, "Ladies and gentlemen, what are we waiting for?"

A man walked onto the stage then from the wings and said, "Gilmor, be patient. A few more minutes and we'll be ready."

I saw Benjamin Zemach walk onto the stage, look around, and then come back into the auditorium.

"That's Benjamin Zemach," I said to Charlotte.

"Oh," she said. "He was the one Jody was talking about. He walks like a dancer."

Is that all she thinks about, I thought to myself, dance this, dance that.

"I heard today," I said, trying to change the subject, "someone say you look just like Katharine Hepburn in *Morning Glory*."

"I hate being told that," she said. "Someone is always telling me that and I hate it."

"I think she's very attractive, Charlotte."

"I don't," she said. "I think she's insipid looking. Did you remember those pictures of Mary Wigman I showed you?"

"Yes."

"Well, that's how I want to look. Her face is like a tragic mask. That's how I want my face to look one day. Like a mask. A tragic mask."

The light dimmed then, the curtain was lowered, the house lights went out completely. There was a pause and the curtain didn't move.

"Ladies and gentlemen, what is wrong?" Gilmor called from the balcony.

The curtain began slowly to move up, and we saw the set, a great terrace in the palace of Herod. It seemed quite beautiful to me. There were a number of young men in costume about the stage, and back of a gigantic staircase was an old cistern surrounded by a wall. The stage was lit very brightly to suggest moonlight. I recognized two of the young actors as being in the class above us at the playhouse, though I had never met either of them.

"That's Joe Anthony and that's Barney Brown," I whispered to Charlotte pointing to them. "They are in the second-year class. Maybe we'll get to be in a play next year."

"I don't want to be in a play. I want to go to Germany and dance."

Finally Salome appeared. It was the mysterious girl I had seen in the patio alone and once with Zemach. She seemed even more beautiful and mysterious onstage.

"I used to see her . . . " I began to say.

"*Shh,*" Charlotte said. "I want to hear the play."

Finally, Herod made his entrance, and Jody Schwartzberg said loud enough that everyone could hear, "That's Lee Cobb."

"He's only twenty-five," I whispered to Charlotte. "He looks much older."

And then that young actor, twenty-five years old, with the authority of a seasoned performer, took over the play and gave it a drive and passion that it had lacked until that moment. How does he do it, I kept saying to myself. How in the world does he do it? Will I ever be that good at twenty-five?

Then came the moment when Salome dances the dance of the seven veils. I was mesmerized by her dancing and her beauty. I looked over at Charlotte, she had her lips in a sneer. She doesn't like it, I thought. Well, to hell with her, I do, and went back to watching.

When the play ended and before the lights were brought up Charlotte said, "I'm going home."

"I'll walk you," I said.

"No, I'll go by myself," she said.

"It's late, you shouldn't be walking home by yourself," I said.

"I'm not afraid," she said. "I just don't want to hear anyone say to me that vulgar display was dancing."

"Didn't you like Herod?" I asked.

"Yes, I did," she said.

"I liked the production," I said. "All of it."

"Well, we have different tastes then," she said. "It is simply not my taste."

"Let's don't quarrel," I said. "And I want to walk you home."

"All right," she said finally. "But let's get out fast."

We walked out then as quickly as we could. Jody Schwartzberg was surrounded by a number of students and I could tell the way they were gesturing they were very impressed by the production as I had been.

"Elizabeth Lynn isn't as yet much of an actress, maybe, but she moves beautifully and she has a wonderful quality onstage," Jody Schwartzberg said as we passed.

"And she's beautiful," someone else said.

The night was cool as we left the theater.

"Do you want to go for a soda?" I asked Charlotte.

"No. I want to go home."

She began across Colorado Boulevard at such a terrific pace that I could hardly keep up with her.

"Don't mind me," she said. "I'll get over this. I shouldn't have come. I know I'm very opinionated when it comes to dance."

"But aren't you glad you saw Lee Cobb?" I asked.

"Yes, I guess I am, but you have to understand. Acting really doesn't interest me. It means nothing to me. Dance is everything to me. And when I see on the stage what I saw tonight, I am offended. That is not dance, that is simply not dance, that is posing, posturing."

"Well, maybe that's all she could do," I said. "Maybe she's not a dancer, but an actress dancing."

"Then she shouldn't be dancing. I am offended."

The two years I was there I saw wonderful productions on the main stage, in addition to that of *Salome,* which had offended Charlotte so completely. *The Brothers Karamazov* with Martin Koslick and Hans von Twardowski, two former Reinhardt actors in exile from Germany. Walter Hampden, the renowned Shakespearean actor, played a black man in blackface, in a play by Martin Craven about a zookeeper, Sidney Howard's *Alien Corn. Saint Joan,* with Joseph Anthony as the Dauphin. Thomas Brown

Henry appeared in Molière's *The Imaginary Invalid;* Douglas Montgomery was in *The Playboy of the Western World;* Victor Jory in Lynn Riggs's *Road Side;* and Rosamond Pinchot starred in a play about John Brown.

Just before Thanksgiving we performed the Roman comedy and *Shakuntula.* We did the Roman comedy first and I don't know how anyone else felt, but I felt stupid and miserable. It all seemed forced and pointless to me and I was only glad it was behind me and to know that I would work next time with a new director, Byron Folger. The students watching were polite and kind after the performance, saying general noncommittal things like "good job" or "nice try."

We were to have a long weekend because of Thanksgiving, and most everyone at school, including Charlotte, was leaving Pasadena to be with family or friends. I had been in touch with Aunt Mag and Uncle Walt, too, and they had made arrangements to pick me up at the boardinghouse early Thanksgiving morning and drive me out to Vista. I had planned to stay the weekend and I told the Boss I wouldn't be there for Thanksgiving or the weekend. Charles Robinson was going, too, but she would have Thanksgiving dinner for Mr. Taylor and Monte.

I had been told just before vacation started that I would be in *Liliom* and would play the part of Sparrow. I went to the library to see if they had a copy of the play, but their copies were all out.

My aunt and uncle were to pick me up at eight, so I got up at seven, bathed, shaved, dressed, and packed my suitcase. I had my breakfast at seven thirty, told the Boss, Mr. Taylor, and Monte good-bye and wished them a happy Thanksgiving. I went upstairs for my suitcase and came back down and sat in the living room with Mr. Taylor and listened to the radio.

Eight o'clock came and I went to the door and watched for their car, but there was none in sight. I went out on the porch and sat on the steps. It was a lovely day and I thought of my family at home all busy now at my grandmother's preparing the Thanksgiving meal. I had gotten a letter from my grandmother with a check for Thanksgiving and telling me how she looked forward to seeing me at Christmas. I wanted to go to the phone and call and wish them a happy Thanksgiving, but I knew I shouldn't.

The Boss came to the screen door then.

"What time are your aunt and uncle coming for you?"

"Eight o'clock."

"Well, it's eight thirty now. Are you sure they have the right address?"

"Yes. Anyway, they have my phone number and they can call if they are lost."

The phone rang inside the house just then. I jumped up.

"I bet that's them now," I said, and started in the house.

Monte was answering the phone when I got inside and said it was for the Boss. She went to the phone and I went upstairs to my room.

Nine o'clock came, then ten, then eleven, and no Aunt Mag or Uncle Walt.

I didn't know what to do. Had I gotten it all wrong? I finally decided to call them. I dialed their number and the phone rang and rang. Finally Uncle Walt answered.

"Hello," he said.

"Uncle Walt?"

"Yes."

"This is Horton."

"Yes."

"How are you?"

"Just fine."

"Is Aunt Mag there?"

"No, she's gone to Vista. She left yesterday, she'll be there for a few days."

"Yes, sir. Happy Thanksgiving."

"Same to you, son."

Then I hung up. I felt desolate. I suddenly was overcome with homesickness and missed my family. I was hurt and angered by my aunt and uncle's behavior, and puzzled, too. I wanted to write my mother and father and tell them what had happened, but I thought better of it and instead wrote them my usual, my every-thing-was-fine-and-how-are-you letter. When I finished it I tore it up. John Forsht was the only one I knew staying in town, having dinner at his boardinghouse. I called on the phone and was told he had gone to John Pelletti's for the day. I didn't have John Pelletti's number, so I couldn't call him. The Boss came to me then and asked what had happened and I told her and she said, "You'll have dinner here then with us." I thanked her and said I'd like to.

After dinner I went for a walk to the playhouse to see if anyone I knew was around, but no one was and I came on back to the boardinghouse. Mr. Taylor was asleep on the couch and I went quietly up the stairs to my room. I silently practiced some of my speech exercises for a while, wrote my parents another letter, and thought back over the performance of the Roman comedy. I knew I couldn't go on acting like that. I felt Miss Townsend was helping me, but I didn't think she was helping me fast enough. I thought again about Lee Cobb's performance as Herod, and that he was only twenty-five. You have seven years to be anywhere near as good as he is, I thought. But how? How did he get that good? How could I? Would I ever? I felt desperate.

Monday before school I went by the library and they had *Liliom* for me. I began reading it as I walked to school and finished it sitting in the playhouse patio. My new director, Byron Folger, came onto the patio then and saw me with *Liliom*. He was a small, slight man, balding, with a gentle expression, and when he spoke I thought there was a certain accent in his speech that I couldn't identify. I knew him by sight, but I'd never met him. He stopped when he saw me and walked over to me.

"Good morning," he said. "I'm Byron Folger. What's your name?"

"Horton Foote."

"Did you have a pleasant Thanksgiving?"

"Yessir," I said, lying. "Did you?"

"Oh, yes. I see you're reading *Liliom*. I'm going to direct it. Have you been cast in it?"

"Yessir."

"What part have you been given?"

"Sparrow."

"Very good. You'll enjoy working on that. Did you find the play interesting?"

"Yessir, I did."

"I believe we start rehearsals after lunch."

"I believe so, sir."

"I'll see you then."

"Yessir."

I thought to myself as he went into the theater, That's the nicest man I've ever known. I hope to God he continues that way.

And he did. Rehearsals were a joy to me. We had two casts for *Liliom.* In the one I was in, John Pelletti played Liliom, Mary Virginia Palmer was Julie, Jody Schwartzberg was the Widow, and I was Sparrow. I couldn't wait each day for rehearsals to begin.

The third day of rehearsal he called me over to him and said, "I think you're doing well with the part. Do you have any questions for me?"

"No, sir."

"Well, just continue as you are and you'll be fine."

"Thank you, sir."

That night I wrote my first really truthful letter home telling my mother and father how happy I was in school and how much I liked the part of Sparrow and how I admired our director.

The next morning at my class with Miss Townsend, I was given *Candida* to read. I asked if I should memorize the scene and she said no. "We'll read it with Louise first, then we'll talk about it and start working. Miss Cornell, you know, has had a great success with the part," she continued. "She's coming to Los Angeles with it this spring, I believe. I don't know who is to play her Marchbanks."

I knew by now that Miss Cornell was often referred to by the New York critics as the First Lady of the American Theater much to the disgust of Jody Schwartzberg, who thought Miss Le Gallienne should be given that title.

A rather tall, thin, handsome woman came out of their bedroom then and Miss Townsend called out to her.

"Louise, who is Katharine Cornell's Marchbank, do you know?"

"No, I don't, dear," she said looking at me. "Is this the March-banks I'm to work with?"

"Yes. Horton this is Miss Lorrimor. She'll be your Prossy."

"How do you do, Horton," Miss Lorrimor said.

"How do you do," I said.

"And a very good type for Marchbanks, I think, Blanche."

"I think so," Miss Townsend said.

CHAPTER 4

Eva Le Gallienne

My grandmother arrived in California the day before our Christmas holiday was to begin. She called from Aunt Mag's and said they would pick me up the next morning at ten and drive us out to La Jolla to Aunt Bo's house. I hadn't seen or heard from Aunt Mag or Uncle Walt since Thanksgiving, and I wondered if they would ever explain what happened. I finally had written my mother about their not appearing, because I was afraid she might write Aunt Mag and thank her for having me for Thanksgiving weekend. She wrote back that both she and my grandmother were very puzzled by her behavior as it was so unlike either Aunt Mag or Uncle Walt. Later when I was at La Jolla and my grandmother told Aunt Bo about it, she said she was sure it was because Uncle Walt had gotten on a drunk and

Aunt Mag reacted in a fury, as she always did when that happened, and left for Vista without him, probably saying she was leaving him forever, which she always said but never did. Anyway, when they did arrive promptly with my grandmother to pick me up, they were as gracious as ever and acted like nothing had ever happened. The Boss was anxious to meet my grandmother, so I asked her if she would mind seeing her. She said she would be happy to and Aunt Mag said she would like to come, too.

The Boss was waiting in the living room and had on the dress she usually wore on Sundays and was extremely gracious and cordial to my grandmother and aunt. She asked if they would like to see my room and they said they would and we took them upstairs. I knew my grandmother very well, however, and I sensed she didn't like the room or the boardinghouse. She was very reserved. The Boss asked them if they would like a cup of coffee and they thanked her, but said they had to be on their way and we left.

My grandmother loved flowers and so she was in heaven in California. All the way to La Jolla she saw roses and bougainvillaea in yards that pleased and delighted her.

"I have never seen such beauty as here in California," my grandmother said over and over.

"This is December, Daisy, wait until spring. Then you'll see flowers everywhere."

"I expect," my grandmother said, "but this is lovely enough for me."

"You'll love La Jolla," Aunt Mag said. "It is a paradise. Isn't it, Walt?"

"Yes, Mag," he said. "But not all of California is a paradise."

"No, certainly not," Aunt Mag agreed. "Now, where Bobo lives in Calexico, I swear to you, is a hell hole. It's not liveable most of the year. Desert and nothing but Mexicans."

"I know all about Calexico. I've been to Calexico, remember?" my grandmother said.

"Of course you have," Aunt Mag said. "What a terrible time that was."

The terrible time had been the Christmas of 1924. Aunt Bo's husband, Harry, who owned an insurance agency, had financial losses and committed suicide. My grandmother was sent for and had spent Christmas and the month of January with Aunt Bo and her children.

La Jolla on the California coast was very beautiful and again flowers were everywhere. I thought of Wharton at Christmas. It could be warm sometimes in the eighties, or it could suddenly go down to thirty degrees, but the pecan trees and the chinaberry trees had all lost their leaves by then, and only the oaks retained theirs. The only flowers that persisted these winter months, at least in our yard, were pansies and chrysanthemums. My grandmother couldn't get over the beauty all around her and she just kept saying over and over, "I have never in my life seen anything like this. Never in my life. Never. Never. Never." I had been so busy with my school and rehearsals that I had hardly seen anything of California, except the areas around the playhouse, which were mostly older houses now turned into rooming and boardinghouses, with small yards, and little attention to flowers or shrubs.

Aunt Bo's rented house was on the ocean. She was there to greet us with her two younger children, Harry and Virginia Rose.

Aunt Bo, as handsome as I had remembered her, was a wonderful hostess, and after my drab boardinghouse, everything seemed to me to be especially pleasing. She was in every sense of that time a modern woman. She had taken over the insurance business after the death of her husband and was making a great success of it. My grandmother obviously adored her and to my surprise when Aunt Bo announced that in California women smoked and so did she, and that in her home cocktails were served before meals and wine with dinner, and that she now voted the Republican ticket, my grandmother beamed and said, "That's perfectly all right with me, Bo." I almost fainted, because I knew my Aunt Rosa smoked, but did it behind my grandmother's back, often having to sneak over to our house to have a cigarette. And as for cocktails and wine, knowing all the tragedies my uncles' addictions to alcohol had brought, I didn't think my grandmother would ever sanction drinking of any kind. But she did at Aunt Bo's, not having anything herself, of course. And I think she was pleased and relieved when I said I wouldn't care for anything but a Coca-Cola.

I had sensed somehow there had been some disturbing goings on in Texas with my uncles. Mother had written that my grandmother had some serious asthma attacks before coming here, but looking at her now in her sister's gracious home, the ocean to be seen from almost every room, I was pleased at how very well she looked and how content and happy she seemed. And indeed, for the four months she remained in California she stayed well and happy.

As I had suspected, my grandmother hadn't liked the looks of my boardinghouse or my room. The day before I was to leave La Jolla for Pasadena my grandmother and Aunt Bo said they were taking a suite of rooms in Pasadena to be near me and wanted me to live with them. I thanked them and said I didn't know if I could leave as my landlady, I knew, was counting on me staying for the school term. Aunt Bo said that was nonsense. "From what I hear of the place, the school should never have put you there." I finally agreed to speak to the Boss.

Confrontation is never something I've enjoyed and so the last day in La Jolla and the ride back to Pasadena were filled with dread over the upcoming meeting.

Uncle Walt and Aunt Mag drove me to Pasadena. She spent the whole time describing her Christmas with her children and grandchildren in Vista, telling me over and over the presents each grandchild had been given, what meals were had at what house, and finally how they spent Christmas day, breakfast at Biddy's, present exchanging at Margaret's, Christmas dinner, and "What a feast that was, wasn't that a feast, Walt, at Lizzie's?" It was dark when we drove up to the boardinghouse, and I must say, after the serenity and beauty of La Jolla, it did seem dreary and depressing.

I thanked them for the ride, kissed Aunt Mag good-bye, took my suitcase and went into the boardinghouse. The Boss was on the couch with her eyes closed when I entered. She opened her eyes then and told me not to be concerned, she wasn't sleeping, just resting, and how was my Christmas? Fine, I said, wondering when and how to tell her I wanted to leave, and she must have sensed something wrong for she said, "Are you feeling all right, son," and I said yes, and then I don't know why but I decided then and there to tell her.

"Boss," I began.

"Yes?"

"You met my grandmother."

"Yes. A lovely lady. I hope she liked your room."

"Well . . ."

"What is it, son?"

"You see . . ."

"Yes? Is there something wrong?"

"No. There's nothing wrong. It's just my grandmother and her sister . . ."

"The one I met?"

"No, another sister. The one we stayed with in La Jolla."

"Uh. Huh."

"They're moving to Pasadena in a week or so . . ."

"Oh, that's nice. I'm sure that pleases you."

"Yes, ma'am."

"Where are they living in Pasadena?"

"On Orange Grove."

"Oh. They must have money, son."

"I guess. Anyway . . ."

"Yes."

"You see . . ."

"Yes."

"They want me to live with them."

"When?"

"In two weeks, as soon as they move here."

"Oh."

Her face drained of color. She sat up on the couch, she seemed in a great deal of pain.

"Boss?"

"Yes."

"It's not that I don't like it here. I do like it here."

"But your grandmother doesn't. She doesn't think it's fine enough for you."

"No, she didn't say that."

"Well, does she know that I make my living with my boarders? Does she know I turned down two other students who wanted your room and that the school told me you would be here for nine months? Does she know that?"

"Well . . . "

"Does she know that or not?"

"I don't guess she does."

"Well, then tell her that. Tell her you can't leave. Tell her I am a widow woman with a son to support and that if I lose the income I was counting on for the next four months I don't know what I'll do. Tell her the school guaranteed me that you would stay until the end of the term and I'll see they make good that promise."

She was off the couch by now and went down the hall to her room. I didn't know what to do or say, so I picked up my suitcase and went up the stairs to my room. I unpacked and then called Charlotte to see if she had returned; she hadn't, so I walked down to the Bates house where John Forsht and Bill Roose lived. They weren't home. I was hungry so I went to the fruit market near the playhouse and got a hamburger, but I was so upset by how emotional the Boss was that I couldn't finish it.

When I got to school the next morning Miss Ong asked to see me. I went with her to her office and she was pleasant and asked about my vacation and I told her I had a nice time and how was hers, and she said just fine. There was a pause then and she looked through some papers and finally turned to me, looking very serious.

"Horton . . . "

"Yes, ma'am."

"Your landlady tells me you want to change your boarding-house. You don't like it there?"

"No, ma'am. It's not that. You see, my grandmother is taking a place in Pasadena and she would like me to live with her."

"And you would like that?"

"Yes, ma'am." Miss Ong looked out the window and thought for a moment. Then she turned back to me. "I'm in a very diffi-cult position. Your landlady was promised by us that except for unseen circumstances, you would remain with her for the school year. On the other hand, if your grandmother wants you with her, I can't force you to stay, can I?"

"No, I guess not."

"Let me think it through."

"Thank you."

That afternoon Miss Ong called me back in the office and told me she had worked it out with my landlady and I was free to leave.

The house in which my grandmother and my Aunt Bo had rented rooms was in a very exclusive part of Pasadena with beautifully kept lawns and lots of flowers and palm trees. Not as lush or as exotic as La Jolla but a great contrast to the drabness of Oakland Avenue. Our landlady was Mrs. Alredge, a genteel lady from Maryland, in her early sixties, soft spoken and still quite handsome. She had four children: Helen, who was a nurse; and Louise and Dorothy, working as secretaries in Pasadena; and Andy still in high school.

The Alredge yard, front and back, was very large. There were orange and lemon trees and a few flowers, roses mostly. She apologized often for this lack of flowers, but explained she was no gardener and couldn't afford someone to take care of the yard for her.

Our suite of rooms was on the second floor. A huge room overlooking the backyard was for Aunt Bo and my grandmother, and a small room was mine. The rooms were connected by a bathroom. The backyard was enclosed by a high hedge. I used to go out there to practice my voice exercises at night.

We had been there about three weeks when I went out back as usual and began walking up and down, starting the exercises to strengthen my consonants, going *b,b,b,b,b,* as loud and as precisely as I could, and then *d,d,d,d,d,* again as loud and precisely as I could. When I got to the *t*'s I thought I heard a voice on the other side of the hedge saying something, but then I thought I had imagined it, and went on with my *t*'s, when I heard loud and clear, "I asked a question, and I'd like an answer. Are you ill, do you need help?"

"No, sir," I said. "I'm not ill."

"Then what is going on?" the voice said. "What is going on? I thought you were in pain."

"No, sir. I'm not in pain."

"Then what the hell is wrong with you?" the voice continued getting angrier all the time.

"Nothing is wrong with me, sir. I'm practicing my voice exercises."

"You are doing what?" The voice sounded really angry now.

"I'm practicing my voice exercises. I'm an actor."

"You are a what?"

"I am an actor, studying acting and I am supposed to practice voice exercises."

"Well, go someplace else. People don't carry on like that in this neighborhood. This is a respectable neighborhood."

"Yessir," I said. "I'm sorry."

Mrs. Alredge and Louise were doing the dishes as I came into the kitchen.

"The man next door called out to me and said I couldn't do my voice exercises out there anymore, that this is a respectable neighborhood."

"The old fool," Mrs. Alredge said. "He's a troublemaker, but I guess you'd better do them here in the house from now on."

Jody Schwartzberg announced in early March that Eva Le Gallienne was coming to the Biltmore Theater in Los Angeles to do three Ibsen plays. She advised everyone to go and see them all, but if you could only see one, make it *Hedda Gabler.* That night after supper I was sitting in my grandmother's bedroom and my grandmother asked what I'd like for my birthday, which was soon.

"I can answer that for you, Daisy," Aunt Bo said. "He wants a check, I'm sure."

"Is that what you want?" my grandmother asked.

"No, ma'am. I want a ticket to see Eva Le Gallienne in *Hedda Gabler* at the Biltmore Theater."

"All right, if that's what you want," she answered.

"I want to go, too, Daisy," Aunt Bo said. "Let's all go."

"All right and I'll treat," my grandmother said.

Hedda Gabler was playing the next Friday night and my

grandmother ordered tickets for the three of us and we took the interurban into Los Angeles in time to have dinner before the show.

In the lobby of the theater they were selling copies of Miss Le Gallienne's book *At 33*. I went over to look at a copy and saw a picture of her for the first time, including one of her as Julie in *Liliom*.

The theater was packed. There was a string trio in the orchestra pit that played when the lights in the auditorium were lowered and before the curtain was raised. The orchestra played, as I remember, "Valse Triste." When they quit playing, the audience applauded and the musicians left and there was silence. I had never seen or read an Ibsen play before. I didn't know what to expect, and I was in no way prepared for the reaction I had. The curtain was raised and there was a living room and Tessman's Aunt Julia, and a maid telling us about the newly married Tessmans. Then Hedda Tessman, Miss Le Gallienne, appeared. She was wearing a short skirt, smoking, as I remember, her hair in a short bob and the audience applauded as she entered.

I watched no one else from then on whenever she was on the stage. It was impossible, it seemed to me, not to watch her. She was compelling and brought a kind of restless energy to the part that at times could be frighteningly cruel and at other times she seemed so vulnerable and frightened. I have never forgotten the way she said the word *bored,* or how she insulted her husband's aunt by pretending she thought the aunt's new bonnet belonged to the maid, how she manipulated her friend Thea, how she threatened to burn her hair, how she destroyed Eilert's manuscript, how she reacted to the news of Eilert's death, and how she took the threats of Judge Brock to blackmail her and use her.

How I felt, not knowing what was going to happen, when I heard the pistol shot offstage and I learned she had killed herself. Mind you it is now sixty-seven years since I saw this production, and yet parts of her performance are as vivid to me now as when I first saw them. In a very fundamental way it changed my life. What I saw on the stage that night made me determined from then on to somehow spend my life in the theater.

"How did you like it, Bo?" my grandmother asked.

"I liked it a lot," she said. "Quite a lot. You know what, Daisy? There are two shows tomorrow."

"The same play?" my grandmother asked.

"No," Aunt Bo said. "This is in repertoire with two other plays."

"*A Doll's House* and *The Master Builder*," I said. "All by Ibsen."

"And do you know what I think we should do?" Aunt Bo continued. "I think we should come back with Horton and see them both. I think it's important for him to see these plays."

"Fine with me," my grandmother said. "We'd better get home then, if we're coming back tomorrow."

On the way out my grandmother saw they were still selling Miss Le Gallienne's book. She walked over to the man selling the book and I saw her reach into her purse and get some money and hand it to him and he handed her the book. She brought it over to me and then said, "Happy Birthday."

"Thank you, Baboo," I said. "You don't know what seeing the play meant to me."

"I'm glad you've enjoyed it," she said. "I'm very glad."

I was up and dressed by seven thirty the next morning. I could smell the coffee from the kitchen. I listened to hear if my aunt and grandmother were up and sensed they weren't and went down to the kitchen for a cup of coffee. Helen, the nurse, the oldest of the girls and the most pragmatic, was there. I wish it had been Louise, because she was much warmer and I felt she would appreciate somehow what I felt about the play and the acting I had seen.

"Good morning, Helen," I said as I came into the kitchen.

"You're up early for a Saturday. I thought you always slept late on Saturdays."

"Not this Saturday," I said, hoping she would ask me why not this Saturday so I could talk about the play, but she didn't.

"Want a cup of coffee?" she finally said.

"Thanks."

"Get a cup and I'll pour you one."

"Thanks," I said, "but I can pour it." I got a cup and poured my coffee.

"You all came in late last night. Where were you? Out sight-seeing?"

"No, we went to the theater."

"Oh," she said.

"At the Biltmore in Los Angeles."

"Oh, I've never been there." She opened the door of the refrigerator. "You want some juice?"

"Thank you. We saw a play at the Biltmore."

"Oh," she said. "I've never seen a play. I think I'm going to try and go some time. I have a friend that went to see a play at the playhouse here last month. She said it was pretty good. Not great. She likes movies better."

She poured herself another cup of coffee and after a moment asked me, "Which do you like better? Plays or movies?"

"Plays," I said. "Hands down."

"Why?" she said.

"I don't know, but I do."

"Have you seen more plays or movies?"

"Movies."

"And you like plays better?"

"Yes."

She suddenly became aware that I had on my good clothes, getting ready for Los Angeles once again.

"Why are you all dressed up?" she asked.

"I'm going into Los Angeles."

"Again?" she asked incredulously. "You were just there last night."

"I'm still going again."

"What are you going for?"

"To see a play. As a matter of fact, two plays."

"Two plays? How are you going to do that?" she wondered.

"One in the afternoon and one in the evening," I answered.

"Same play?"

"No, different plays."

"I had a friend once," she said, "every time I went to a movie with her she liked she insisted on sitting and seeing it over again. Once she wanted to see one three times. There's not a movie in the world I could see twice."

Mrs. Alredge came into the kitchen then.

"Helen, you and Horton run on out now. I want the kitchen to myself while I fix breakfast."

Helen went out into the backyard and I went into the living room. I could hear my aunt and grandmother moving around overhead in their room. I was relieved to know they were up.

*   *   *

We saw *A Doll's House* at the matinee and *The Master Builder* in the evening. Josephine Hutchinson was Nora in *A Doll's House* and Le Gallienne was in the lesser role of Mrs. Linde. I remember liking Josephine Hutchinson and the play and being interested in seeing Miss Le Gallienne in a supportive role, but it wasn't until that evening's performance of *The Master Builder* that I really was again completely taken in by the play and her performance as Hilda. So different than her Hedda, young, impulsive, demanding, in her uncompromising way, physical acts of courage from Solness that finally destroyed him and when she learns of his death after attempting what she asked of him, her moment of quiet elation, saying the words of Ibsen: "But he mounted right to the top. And I heard harps in the air." Then as I remember it, with almost religious fervor, saying, "My—my Master Builder." She seemed so different to me in all these parts, and yet there was an essence that was always unmistakably hers. And the Ibsen plays moved me in a way no plays had before. Most plays, I realized after seeing these, were thin gruel, of little substance.

I was at the playhouse early Monday morning and the first to arrive. I knew the route Charlotte took to school so I started toward her boardinghouse. I no sooner had crossed Colorado Boulevard when I saw Charlotte in the distance. I waved to her and she began to run toward me. I could see she was happy about something.

"What is it?" I called out to her. "What is it?"

She didn't answer until she reached me, out of breath.

"Look what was waiting for me at home this weekend?"

She showed me a booklet all in German, but with pictures of dancers and I saw one of Mary Wigman.

"That's Mary Wigman," I said.

"Yes, it is. You're learning. It's in German," she said. "I'm learning German so I can speak to Mary Wigman when I go to Germany. This is a catalogue of her school. It arrived yesterday. And guess what?"

"What?"

"My parents told me that if I finished here next year and I still wanted to go and study in Germany and if I worked and helped get the money, they would give me permission to go."

"That's wonderful, Charlotte. I'm happy for you."

She took the picture of Mary Wigman from me and kissed it.

"Look what I have," I said. "I went to Los Angeles over the weekend and I saw Eva Le Gallienne in three Ibsen plays and this is her autobiography."

"Oh," she said taking the book and looking at it for a few minutes and then handing it back to me. "Were the plays interesting?"

"Oh, yes. I think you would have liked them. You should try to go. They are here next weekend. I'd like to go back."

"No, I can't do anything like that. I must save every penny now, so I can get to Germany."

We were at the playhouse by then and I saw Jody Schwartzberg.

"Jody," I called out to her. "Guess what happened to me this weekend? I saw all three of the Le Gallienne plays and this is her autobiography," holding the book up for her to see.

"Oh," she said taking the book and glancing at it. "I'm going next weekend."

"She's wonderful, Jody," I said. "It is my ambition now to get to New York and be part of her company one day."

"That'll never happen," she said. "Not with your diction. Why, even the people that answer the phone at the Civic Repertory Theater have perfect diction," and with that she handed my book back to me and walked off.

At night in my room I could hear Aunt Bo and my grandmother talking. My grandmother felt she should return to Texas by the end of April. Aunt Bo was trying to get her to stay in Pasadena longer, and one night I heard her suggest that my grandmother should sell her house in Wharton and move to California. I didn't like to hear that, as I couldn't imagine my grandmother not living in Wharton. That night I began to not feel well. I was seldom sick and I thought a good night's sleep would take care of whatever was bothering me, but in the morning I had a severe stomachache. It concerned me and I didn't feel like going to school, but wanted to stay in bed and sleep. I called out to my grandmother and she came into my room and I told her I wasn't feeling well and didn't think I'd go to school that day and would she call Miss Ong and tell her I'd be there tomorrow. Aunt Bo was in the room then and she asked me what was the matter, and I said I didn't know, but I had a stomachache and I guess I ate something last night that didn't agree with me, and Aunt Bo said we all ate the same thing, and we're not affected. Then she came over to me in the bed and felt my forehead to see if I had any temperature.

"Daisy, I don't think he has fever," she said to my grandmother. "Here, feel his forehead and see what you think."

My grandmother felt my forehead then and she said, "I really can't tell, Bobo. Stick out your tongue, son."

I stuck out my tongue and she and Aunt Bo looked at it. "It's not coated," my grandmother said. "Does your stomach hurt you, son?"

"Yes, ma'am."

"Where?" Aunt Bo asked.

"Here." I pointed to where the pain seemed most acute.

My grandmother felt my forehead again.

"I swear I think he does have a little fever, Bobo."

Then Aunt Bo felt my head again.

"Maybe so," she said. She took my wrist and felt my pulse. "Do you feel at all nauseated, son?"

"No, ma'am."

"Do you feel feverish?" my grandmother asked.

"I don't think so. I feel a little warm though."

"I'll see if Mrs. Alredge has a thermometer," Aunt Bo said and left the room.

"Baboo," I said.

"Yes, darling."

"Would you please call the school for me now?"

"All right. Who do I speak to?"

"Miss Ong."

"All right."

She went into her room and I could hear very faintly her talking to someone at the school. I looked at my watch and it was eight thirty and the students would be making their way toward the school. I began to practice my vowel sounds in the bed— *a,e,i,o,u.* At first I did them normally. Then I began to elongate them and I was in the middle of an elongated *o* when my grandmother came back in.

"I spoke to Miss Ong. She seems very nice. She said to stay in bed and rest and to please keep in touch as she was concerned."

Aunt Bo came in then, followed by Mrs. Alredge and Helen. Helen had a thermometer. She gave it to my grandmother. My grandmother gave it a good shake and said, "Open your mouth, honey," and I did so and she put the thermometer in my mouth and looked at her watch to time how long it was to stay.

Once my grandmother felt the thermometer had been in my mouth long enough she took it out and looked at it.

"Well, he has a fever," she said.

"How much?" Aunt Bo asked, walking over to look at the thermometer.

"A hundred and one," my grandmother said.

Helen came over to me on the bed.

"Do you have any pain?" she asked.

"Yes, I do."

"How much?"

"Well, not a lot, but I have pain."

"Let me see where the pain is." She came over to me and began to press my stomach with her hand. "Don't worry," she said. "I won't hurt you. Just tell me when I press where it's most sore." As she pressed various parts of my stomach she asked, "Does that hurt?"

"Not there," I said the first time she pressed.

"Does that hurt?" as she pressed again.

"Not much."

"What do you mean, not much?" she asked.

"Well, that's what I mean. It hurts a little, but not much."

She pressed again and this time I didn't say anything but I winced with pain.

"I take it that hurts," she said.

"Yes, it does," I said.

"I think we should get him to a doctor right away," Helen said. "It could be appendicitis."

"Oh, mercy," my grandmother said.

"Now, Daisy," Aunt Bo said. "Just keep calm. It may not be serious at all. Let's just get him to the doctor."

"Right away," my grandmother said. "Right away." She turned to Helen then. "My husband's brother died of a ruptured appendix. He was in his fifties and a brilliant lawyer. Ruptured. His appendix ruptured."

"Now, Daisy, just keep calm. We have the finest doctors in the world here. He'll get proper attention right away."

Mrs. Alredge came back in.

"How's the patient?" she said.

"He has appendicitis," my grandmother said.

"Now, Daisy, you don't know that," Aunt Bo said trying to calm her down.

"You heard what Helen said."

"I didn't say he had it, Mrs. Brooks. I only said he should go to a doctor as it might be appendicitis."

"I'm scared to death of appendicitis," my grandmother said to Mrs. Alredge. "My late husband's brother died with a ruptured appendix. Do you know a good doctor?"

"Indeed, I do," Mrs. Alredge said. "I'll call and make an appointment."

The appointment was for eleven o'clock. Helen said she'd take off from work and drive us. I slowly dressed, and wondered what it would mean if I did have appendicitis. I didn't want to ask my grandmother because I could see she was already beside herself with worry, so when she went to her room to get dressed, I motioned to Aunt Bo to come close to me so my grandmother couldn't hear my question.

"What does it mean if I have appendicitis?"

"Now, you may not have it," she said.

"But what if I do?"

"Then they'll operate on you and remove your appendix."

"How much school will I have to miss?"

"I don't know," she said.

Helen came back into the room then.

"We'd better get going," she said. "Come on. Lean on me while we go down the stairs."

"I can walk," I said.

"Well, walk carefully."

The doctor was ready to see me when I got to his office. Helen knew him and introduced him to me and my aunt and grandmother. His nurse came in then and she was introduced to all of us.

"I hear you have a little pain in your stomach," the doctor said.

"Yessir."

"Have you had any pain like this before?"

"No, sir."

"When did it start?"

"Very early this morning. I woke up with it."

"I see. All right. Let's go into my office and I'll take a look at you and see what we can find out."

He went into his office and stood by the door as the nurse went in and I followed her, and then he closed the door.

I was scared all of a sudden, and suddenly I felt weak and my hands began to tremble.

The doctor must have sensed my fear for he said in the calmest kind of way, "Don't be afraid, son. I'm not going to hurt you. I'm just going to examine you for a little, to see if we can find out what is upsetting your stomach."

"Yessir," I said.

He asked me to take off my shirt and to unbutton my pants, which I did and then he got his stethoscope and listened to my heart, I guess. Then the nurse brought over a thermometer and asked me to open my mouth and I did and she put the thermometer in my mouth, and looked at her watch to time it. No one was talking and it was so quiet in the office I could hear my own breathing. The nurse took the thermometer out of my mouth and looked at it and then showed it to the doctor. Neither said anything and the doctor asked me to lie down on the examining table. He began to press my stomach, asking if this hurt and that hurt and I would tell him when it hurt and how much. After a few minutes of that he told me to get off the table and to put my shirt back on, and I did and he said that would be all and he opened the door and asked to speak to my grandmother.

She went into his office and he closed the door. I went out to Aunt Bo and Helen, and after a few minutes my grandmother came out with the doctor.

"He does have a slight case of appendicitis," my grandmother said. "But the doctor feels it's not serious enough to operate, but if it ever flares up again, he should have an operation." She turned to me then and said, "He thinks you should rest today and tomorrow and not go back to school until Wednesday."

By the next morning the pain was all gone and I wanted to go back to school, but my grandmother insisted I stay in bed for another day and so I did. The next day, though, I was up very early as I had a lesson with Miss Townsend and I was out of the house by seven thirty and feeling fine.

My friends at school were all glad to see me and there was a note from Miss Ong asking me to come and see her after lunch.

Charlotte and I went for a walk during lunch as she was not having lunch either as she was saving her money now for her eventual trip to Germany and the Wigman School.

"Miss Ong wants to see me after lunch," I said. "I wonder why?"

"She was seeing a number of us yesterday to tell us whether we were being asked back for the second year or not."

"You mean you have to be asked back?"

"Yes."

"You got asked back, I take it."

"Yes, but I don't want to come back. I'll tell you a secret, but swear you won't tell anyone else."

"I swear."

"My parents say if I get a job this summer and save my money, I don't have to come back here; I can go to Germany instead in the fall."

"Oh, I'm happy for you, Charlotte."

"Thank you."

"But I'll miss you."

"I'll miss you, too. If I write to you, will you write back to me?"

"I surely will."

"Someday I'm going to be a great dancer, you know. I feel that."

"I know you do. I wish I felt that confident about my acting."

"You'll get confidence."

"Suppose I don't get asked back?"

"You will. John Forsht works in the office, you know, and he told me he saw your name on a list of students being asked back."

"That's a relief."

Miss Ong made it official that I was asked back, and I thanked her. She said that Miss Townsend felt I was making real progress. I thanked her for telling me that, too.

"And I suppose you are planning to come back, aren't you?"

"Yes, ma'am. I certainly am."

"There's to be a third year, too, you know. It's starting next year. Mr. Brown has a marvelous program outlined for the third-year students. He has leased a theater in Padua Hills and they will spend the whole year doing plays. Jerry Corey is to direct. He's very gifted. There will be only a select number chosen for the third-year group. Joseph Anthony, Barney Brown, Beatrice Newport, Patricia Coates. I'm sure you have seen them around and in the plays on the main stage."

"Oh, yes, ma'am."

"All of the invited ones will be of that caliber. The first play of the season will be *The Sea Gull* by Chekhov. So, you see when you come back next year, if you work hard, perhaps you'll be invited for the third year. Wouldn't that be thrilling?"

"Yes, ma'am."

A week later there was a crisis in Texas involving one of my uncles and my grandmother felt she had to go back. I sensed she didn't want to go, but off she went. Aunt Bo left at the same time and I was alone with the Alredges.

CHAPTER 5

Caney Valley Hospital

We were to begin rehearsals for the final plays of the year and this time they were to be presented, without scenery or lights, on the main stage at the playhouse on an afternoon before invited guests.

I can't for the life of me remember the name of the play I was cast in, nor the name of the other plays. I do remember thinking the essence of my character was not unlike the character of the Sparrow in *Liliom,* and that I felt very secure in my playing of it. I was sorry my grandmother wasn't there to see me. I called Aunt Mag but she and Uncle Walt were busy and couldn't come. She told me that she had promised my grandmother that they would come for me when school was over and take me to the bus station.

When I got back to my room later that afternoon I found a letter from my mother. She wrote that my brother Tom Brooks had an attack of appendicitis, too. A mild attack like mine, but that Dr. Toxie and Dr. Green Davidson had said, though it wasn't serious, an appendix was as useless as tonsils, and had urged my mother and father to have my brother's removed. They agreed and he was operated on. It was all over now and he was fine and up and about.

The day before school was to end I asked Charlotte if I could take her out to dinner. She said she would go, but she wanted to pay for herself. We argued about that for a while and she finally agreed to my paying. I had a little extra money, because Aunt Bo, just before leaving, said, "Give me your hand, Horton," and I held out my hand and she put a ten-dollar bill there.

Charlotte and I went to a restaurant that charged ninety-nine cents for dinner, and advertised that you could have as many helpings as you wanted. John Pelletti had gone there with his parents and said it was very good and it was true about getting as much as you wanted as he'd had three pieces of pie.

Charlotte already had a job for the summer working as a waitress. She hoped to leave for Germany in the early fall. Again we promised to write each other and she talked about being a great dancer. I had read somewhere about Harold Kroutzberg, another German dancer, and I asked her about him and she said she had read about him, but he was considered pale next to Wigman. Wigman, she said, had great, great power, and she couldn't believe that in three months she'd be in her classes and able to see her dance and maybe, in time, dance with her.

We said good-bye to each other that night, as she was leaving early the next morning for home and would not be in school for the last day. Again, we promised to write each other and she gave me her home address and I gave her mine. I stood in the yard of her boardinghouse and watched as she went up the front stairs. As she reached the door, she turned and spoke to me in German and then went into the boardinghouse.

I wrote to her once from Texas while she was still in California. She wrote me back and said she was leaving in ten days for Germany, and when she got there she would send me her address. She never did.

My cousin Nannie was waiting for me at the bus station when I arrived in Houston. I came off the bus with my shoes in my hand. I had taken them off somewhere in New Mexico, I explained to Nannie, and because of the heat my feet had swollen and I couldn't get them back on.

All the way back to Wharton, Nannie talked about my uncles. She said their behavior was killing my grandmother, and she was afraid their extravagances were going to bankrupt her. My Uncle Brother was now a seaman going God knows where, and had deserted his wife and child. My Uncles Billy and Speed, after getting into one scrape after another, were in Houston the last she heard, supposedly looking for work, but probably drinking themselves into oblivion. My grandmother, she said, "had come back from California looking well and happy but after a few weeks trying to cope with one escapade after another of her sons, each more horrendous than the last, had lost weight, had constant asthma attacks, and was in bed now most of the time. "Your Father," she continued, "looks depressed and unhappy most of the time, too, and worries about the tenants renting your house. He told me he couldn't wait to move back, but your mother feels they can't leave your grandmother now."

"How is my daddy's business?" I asked.

"I think there is none. You can't give cotton away, you know," she said gloomily.

"I thought they had such a good crop last year and the prospects were good this year," I said.

"Yes, I guess they picked a lot of cotton, but there is no price for it. So some of the farmers say they feel like just leaving it in the fields." She sighed then and pointed to some convicts working in the cotton fields in the penitentiary outside of Sugar Land. "Look at those poor devils," she said. "How would you like to spend your life doing that?"

"I wouldn't like it, thank you," I said.

"How was California?" she said.

"Fine. I like it."

"Is it as pretty as everyone says? Your grandmother said she'd never seen such flowers. She told my mother that her sisters were trying to get her to sell her house and move out there. Well, I said in my opinion that's just running away from your troubles and you can't do that, you know. Your troubles will follow you wherever you go—California, Texas. Did you see any movie stars in California?"

"A few around the playhouse. Onslow Stevens, Victor Jory, Gloria Stuart, and Douglas Montgomery."

"They're not real movie stars," my cousin said. "Not like Joan Crawford or Norma Shearer."

"I guess not," I agreed. "But they got their start at the playhouse, so they still come around. Douglas Montgomery did a play there."

There were cotton fields almost all the way to Wharton. In some of the fields the cotton was blossoming and in others the blossoms were gone and replaced by squares.

Nannie began again on my uncles and their escapades, and I was getting more and more depressed by her stories, so I tried to change the subject.

"Are there going to be any dances at the opera house?"

"Red Cornelson played there last week."

"Did you go?"

"No, Bolton had to work. I heard they had a very small turnout. Did you go to a lot of dances in California?"

"No. Not a one."

"Not a one?"

"No."

"Mercy. What do you do for entertainment?"

"Well, they kept us pretty busy, but when I had some free time I'd go see plays."

"That's all you did?"

"Yes."

"Mercy. The little theater here now has been temporarily disbanded. Did your mother write you that?"

"No. Why?"

"You know how people are in this one-horse town. You can't keep them interested in anything. They say they're starting up in the fall, but I'll believe it when I see it. You ought to come back here and run the little theater."

"That will be the day."

We were in the outside of Wharton now. I looked around at the familiar houses coming up: Mr. Billy Neal's house, and across the road, Mrs. "Bucky" Neals, and farther down the road, Sue Rowans. After crossing the Santa Fe Railroad tracks I could see in the distance to the right of the road the cotton gin. Then Mrs. Taylor's house, Mr. and Mrs. Taylor were sitting on the porch and waving as we passed, then the Alday house, and then the former Cookenboo house.

"Does anyone ever hear from Mrs. Cookenboo?"

"I think your grandmother keeps in touch with her," Nannie said. "The last I heard she was living in Houston with John B. and his wife, Ada. You heard she got married, didn't you?"

"Mrs. Cookenboo?"

"Yes."

"No."

"Well, I guess your grandmother didn't want you to hear about it. She told your grandmother that she met this nice Baptist preacher in Houston and was going to marry him."

"But Mrs. Cookenboo was a Methodist, I thought."

"She was and is, but I think she was unhappy living with John B. and Ada. She couldn't get along with Elwood's wife, Bennie, so I figured she thought she'd try marrying her a preacher, but it didn't work out. He turned out to be senile. She is back with John B. and Ada the last I heard, unless she's found another preacher."

We were pulling into the driveway of my grandmother's house now, and I could see behind it the back of my house and its backyard. It seemed strange to be going to my grandmother's house first and not my own. My mother must have heard the car pull into the driveway for she and my two brothers were waiting on the porch to greet me as I crossed the yard. My mother seemed unchanged, and my brothers, grown taller, came down the porch stairs to take my suitcase from me. Nannie came up on the porch with me and watched as I kissed and embraced my mother and shook my brothers' hands.

"Where's Baboo?" I asked.

"She's inside resting," my mother said.

We all went inside the house to my grandmother's bedroom and she was lying in her big Victorian bed and looked very frail to me.

"Hello, honey," she said. "Did you have a nice trip?"

"It was awful hot, Baboo," I said as I bent over to kiss her.

"Did Mag and Walt take you to the bus station?"

"Yes, they sure did," I said.

"I'll never get over the way they acted Thanksgiving day."

"How did they act Thanksgiving day?" Nannie wanted to know.

"Well, they told him they were coming for him Thanksgiving day and were going to take him to Vista to spend the weekend with their children and they never showed up, never called or anything. Just didn't show up and the poor child was sitting there practically all day waiting for them."

"What happened?" Nannie wanted to know. "Did they just forget?"

"No, they didn't forget," my grandmother said. "Mag's husband, Walt, drinks and my sister Bo thinks he got on a drunk just before Thanksgiving and Mag went off to her children without him."

"Did they ever explain or apologize?" Nannie asked.

"Not a peep," my grandmother said. "Not a peep."

"Didn't you ever ask her what happened?"

"No, I didn't want to embarrass her," my grandmother said.

"I would have asked her," Nannie said.

"I want to go downtown and say hello to Daddy," I said.

I really just wanted to get away from looking at my grandmother, because I couldn't believe the change in her since California. There she was energetic and outgoing and cheerful. She looked suddenly so old and helpless in that enormous bed of hers.

"Don't go just yet, son," she said. "Tell me how the Alredges were?"

"They all seemed fine. They sent their love to you."

"Who are the Alredges?" Nannie asked.

"The owners of the house that we had rooms in."

"She's a very admirable woman," my grandmother said. "She's had a lot to bear, but she never complains. Her husband deserted her ten years ago and left her with three girls and a boy to raise. I think she has a very hard time managing even now, poor thing." She sighed and closed her eyes.

"I think we better go now," my mother said. "We don't want to tire you, Mama."

My grandmother didn't ask us to stay this time, so I kissed her again, on her forehead this time.

My father was standing in the front of his store when Nannie and I drove up in her car. He came over as I got out of the car and we gave each other a hug. I thanked Nannie for bringing me and she drove off and my father and I stood on the sidewalk in front of the store talking.

"Glad to be home, son?" my father asked me.

"Yessir," I said.

"Well, things are different now, son, a whole lot different. Your uncles have just about driven your grandmother crazy."

"Yessir. She looks terrible."

"I don't know how much longer she can go on this way."

"What do you mean, Daddy?" I asked.

"I mean . . ." and he became quite angry now. "Their behavior is sending her nearer to the grave every day. Faster and faster." He paused then and sighed and walked into the store and I followed him. "We moved over there so your mother could see to them while she went to California, to get away from them, and they were pretty good for a while, but the minute she got back, Billy and Speed both went on benders. Your Uncle Brother is on a ship. I guess you know that."

"Yessir."

"He's not worth killing, either, son. I hate to say that, because I was always fond of him when he was growing up, but I swear he's just not worth killing now. And I'll tell you this, son, I'd do anything for your grandmother, but I don't want to go on living in her house any longer. I want to go back to our own house. I miss my house."

"Yessir."

Hoping to change the subject as I was getting more depressed by the minute by his accounts of my grandmother and my uncles, I asked, "How is the cotton crop?"

He gave a long, heavy sigh, and I realized I had again chosen the wrong subject.

"Cotton," he said, "is in a terrible slump. I feel so sorry for the farmers. They work in those fields from early morning until dark and what does it get them? Nothing. They can't give their cotton away. Can't give it away."

Thank heavens a customer came in then and wanted to buy some work clothes. My father always brightened up when faced with a customer, and suddenly looked like a man on top of the world with no cares at all.

I had been given the sun parlor for my bedroom while we lived at my grandmother's. I was delighted to be there as it was my favorite room in the house. It was surrounded by windows, which were kept up, so that if there was a breeze anywhere, we got our share of it.

The third night I was home I was awakened by pain in my stomach like the one I had experienced in Pasadena. I tried to get back to sleep, but I couldn't. In a few minutes the pain increased and I called out to my brother Tom Brooks where he was sleeping in the next room. He didn't hear me, but my grandmother did and called out asking what was wrong.

I didn't want to worry her so I said, "Nothing, I just want to speak to my mother."

"Horton," my grandmother said, "I'm no fool and if you want to speak to your mother at twelve o'clock at night something is wrong."

"Yes, ma'am. My stomach is hurting me again."

"Like in Pasadena?" she asked.

"Yes," I said. "Only worse."

"Oh, my God," she said and then called as loud as she could, "Hallie!" Then even louder, "Hallie!"

I could hear the door of my mother's room opening and her sleepy voice saying, "Yes, Mama. What is it?"

"It's Little Horton. He's having another attack of appendicitis."

"Oh, Mama. No," she said.

I could hear my father now.

"What's wrong?"

"It's Little Horton," my grandmother said. "Appendicitis."

"Oh, my God," my father groaned.

By this time, my mother had come into my room and over to my bed.

"Are you in pain, son?"

"Yes, ma'am. Pretty much," I said.

"Call Toxie, Hallie," I heard my grandmother call out from her room.

"Yes, Mama. I will," my mother answered back.

"Remember your Uncle Billy," my grandmother called out again.

"Yes, Mama," my mother said and went off to the phone.

Both of my brothers were awake by now and I heard them asking my father, who was in the room by now, "What about Uncle Billy?"

"Never mind about your Uncle Billy," my father said. "Anyway, it wasn't your Uncle Billy, it was your Great Uncle Billy."

"He's dead, isn't he?" my brother John Speed asked.

"Yes, he is," my father said.

"I know about him," my brother Tom Brooks said. "They told me about him when I was in the hospital after I had my appendix out. He had a ruptured appendix before the doctor could get to him and it killed him. That's how Rudolph Valentino died, too, they told me when I was in the hospital."

"Will you hush up, son," my father said and he sounded angry. "Just be quiet. Your brother needs to be quiet and rest."

He came into my room and over to my bed. "How do you feel, son?" he asked.

"A little better," I said.

"Pain all gone?" he asked hopefully.

"No, not all gone."

"Well, I'll bet it'll be gone before long."

"I hope so."

My mother came into the room then. "I got Toxie. He'll be right over."

My grandmother called out from her room. "Did you get Toxie?"

"Yes, Mama."

"What did he say?"

"He said he'd be right over."

"Did you tell him he has appendicitis?"

"No, I didn't, Mama, because I don't know if he has it."

"I think he has."

"Well, we'll soon find out, Mama."

The front doorbell rang then and my father went to answer it. My mother had pulled a chair up beside my bed and was sitting on it and holding my hand. Dr. Toxie, always very quiet and calm, and my father came into the room.

"Hello, son," Dr. Toxie said. "How was California?"

"Pretty good, sir," I said.

"Have you gotten into the movies, yet?"

"No, sir," I said, trying to smile.

"Have a little pain?"

"Yessir."

"In your stomach area?"

"Yessir."

"Your mother tells me you had something like this in California?"

"Yessir."

"And the doctor said it was appendicitis?"

"Yessir, and then it went away."

"I see."

My grandmother had gotten out of bed by now and came into the room dressed in her robe.

"Hello, Toxie," she said.

"Hello, Mrs. Brooks," he said.

"Did he tell you about the attack in Pasadena?"

"Yes."

"Did Little Horton tell you that the doctor there said if he had another attack, it should be taken out?"

"No," Toxie said, calm as ever. "He didn't tell me that."

"I had mine taken out, Horton," Tom Brooks said. "And there is nothing to it."

"Would you turn on some more lights now please, so I can examine him."

The lights were turned on and he had me remove my pajama top and undo my pajama pants. He got out of his doctor's bag a stethoscope and a thermometer. He examined me first with the stethoscope and then asked me to open my mouth and took my temperature. I looked over at my grandmother and still couldn't believe this was the same person that not more than a month ago was in California with Aunt Bo going to beauty parlors, buying clothes, looking happy, and dressing as fashionably as Aunt Bo. I couldn't stand seeing her look so frail and helpless.

Dr. Toxie took the thermometer out of my mouth, looked at it, and along with the stethoscope put it away in his bag. Then he bent over me and began pressing my stomach. I wish I could have said I wasn't in pain, but I was and told him so. After a moment or so Dr. Toxie stopped his pressing and said could he speak to my mother and father alone. My grandmother sat beside me then, holding my hand.

"Are you in pain, darling?" she asked.

"Some," I said.

"As bad as in California?"

"Just about the same."

Mother came to the door of the sun parlor then. "Mama," she called. "Could you come with us?"

"Certainly," my grandmother said and went out of the room.

Tom Brooks and John Speed had stretched out on the floor to rest and were both sound asleep.

I started thinking of Charlotte and wondered what she was up to, and wondered if I could ever obtain the same confidence that she seemed to have. I looked out the sun parlor window then to the back of our house and there was a light on there, and I wondered if the tenants were taking good care of the house. Mother had told me that morning that my grandmother was now thinking of moving to Houston to stay with my Aunt Rosa, as she had to work and was having difficulty finding help to stay with her baby daughter. I told Mother that Aunt Bo wanted my grandmother to move to California and live, and I thought she was happy out there.

"She was happy," my mother said, "and carefree, but she felt guilty, too."

"Why?" I asked.

"Because she felt she was needed back here and she needs to feel needed and useful she told me, and Rosa does need her now and badly. She will get a house now in Houston it looks like, and hire a maid to do the cooking and then Rosa can go to work with a clear conscience."

"What about the boys?" I asked.

"Billy and Speed are in Houston, as you know, supposedly looking for work," she said. "They will live with Mama, too, I suppose. She will sell this house, she says, no matter whether she goes to California or Houston, unless your father will let her give it to us."

"Do you think he would accept it, Mother?"

"No, he says he won't and I don't think he will ever change his mind because he says the boys will always feel they can come back here and have a place to stay if it belongs to us. And he wants to be free of the boys."

"And what do you feel, Mother?"

"I am perfectly content with the house we have."

Mother and Daddy came back into the room then and came over to me.

"Son," Mother began ever so hesitantly. "Dr. Toxie says it is appendicitis, but he doesn't think at this time it needs operating on, so he has gone to the ice house and is sending back a block of ice and Daddy and I will keep ice packs on you until in the morning. Dr. Toxie thinks that will reduce the swelling and the pain and by breakfast time the pain should all be gone. He suggested, though, that you rest in bed tomorrow and he'll come over in the early afternoon and take another look at you."

"Yes, ma'am."

My grandmother came in then with a towel wrapped around crushed ice and gave it to my father. "There's still a little ice left in the icebox. It will last fine until Toxie gets the other ice here," she said.

"Thank you, Baboo," my father said and took the towel filled with ice and placed it on my stomach.

"You go back to bed, Mama," Mother said. "There's nothing else to be done now."

"I can't sleep now, honey. I'm wide awake," my grandmother said.

"I know, Mama, but get in bed and rest anyway."

"All right." She went reluctantly on back to her room.

"And you try to sleep, son," my mother said.

"I can't sleep, Mama," I said.

"Well, close your eyes and try."

"All right." I closed my eyes for a moment and then I opened them and looked over at my mother. She had her eyes closed but not to sleep. I knew she was praying.

"Hon," my father said. "Get some more ice, please. This is about gone."

She got up and left the room and I closed my eyes and tried to sleep.

"Is this ice helping at all, son?" my father asked.

"Not so far," I said.

"Well, we have to give it a little time, Toxie said. He was sure it would help in time."

"Yessir."

I closed my eyes again and I heard my mother come back into the room.

"Is he asleep?" she whispered.

"I don't know," my father whispered back.

I kept my eyes closed while my father took one towel off and put another towel with fresh ice on.

"I pray this is going to help," Mother whispered.

"Toxie said it would."

"I know."

"I just can't, honey, afford another operation now if it can possibly be avoided. I still haven't been able to pay Toxie for Tom Brooks's operation."

My grandmother came back into the room. Mother motioned to her, evidently to be quiet, for when she spoke, it, too, was in a whisper.

"Is he feeling better?"

"I don't know," my mother whispered back. "He's asleep."

"Well, that's a good sign," my grandmother said. "If he was in pain he couldn't sleep."

The doorbell rang then.

I heard my father say, "You hold the towel, hon, I'm going to let the ice man in."

I felt him withdraw the towel and then felt Mother putting it back on my stomach. It did feel good having it there, and I thought it was helping, but suddenly the pain began to increase and I began to moan. It was as if something was taking over my body that I couldn't control, and I wanted to stop the severe pain but I couldn't and I didn't want to moan and frighten my mother and grandmother, but I couldn't control that, either. There was a pain then so sharp I thought I would die and then it subsided and I thought, It is over now, the pain will go.

But my mother was screaming now, "Hon, hon, call Toxie. He is in terrible pain. Call Toxie." My brothers awakened then and I heard Tom Brooks say sleepily, "What's going on?"

"*Shh, shh,*" my mother said.

"All I can think of, Hallie, is your Uncle Billy," my grandmother said.

"Mama, please don't."

I opened my eyes then and I saw my father come into the room.

"I called Toxie. He'll be right over. He said keep on the ice packs until he gets here."

"I know your business is slow now, son," my grandmother said to my father. "And if there is to be an operation, I want to help pay for it."

"I don't want your help, Baboo, thank you. We'll manage," my father said.

"I know, but—" my grandmother began again.

"Now, Mama, please," my mother said. "We'll talk about this another time."

I had another sudden seizure of pain. I said to myself, I won't moan and I won't scream, I won't, but I did scream and John Speed was frightened by my screams and he began to cry and I saw my grandmother comforting him and I screamed once more and this time I said, "Help me, please somebody help me. I'm in pain, I'm in such pain."

"Be still, honey," my mother said, "so I can keep the ice packs on you."

I tried to keep still but the pain began again and I screamed again and Dr. Toxie came in the room then and he came over to me and said, "Let's get him to the hospital right away before his appendix ruptures."

"Shall he go in his pajamas?" my mother asked.

"Yes, just let's go. Let's help him up out of the bed." He took me by the shoulders and said, "Horton, try to help us. We have to get you to the hospital as soon as possible. Your father will help me and we'll be as gentle as possible, but you have to help us by letting us help you." He slowly lifted me up and said to my father, "Hold him in this position."

My father took hold of me then and held me while Dr. Toxie took hold of my legs and gently, but firmly, moved them off the bed, then he held me under my arms while he raised me up. My father then held one side of me and Toxie the other and they started slowly walking me out of the room. The pain lessened, and I was going to tell the doctor that, but I suddenly felt dizzy and like I was going to faint, so I just concentrated on not fainting. They slowly got me outside and into Dr. Toxie's car. They put me in the backseat and Dr. Toxie told me to stretch out if I wanted to. The hospital was only three blocks away. I thought to myself, Who would ever have thought I would be going to the hospital with appendicitis in the middle of the night? I could see a very pale moon in the sky, and every now and then a big white cloud passing over it, blotting it out.

The Wharton Hospital was a large two-story house that had been bought by Dr. Toxie Davidson and his father, Dr. Green Davidson, to use as a hospital. I had never been inside it, but the outside looked like many two-story houses in Wharton. It had galleries in front of the first floor and in front of the second floor. Dr. Toxie's wife, Louise, had died there in childbirth a few years before.

I could see the hospital up ahead now and the car stopped in front and Dr. Toxie and my father helped me out of the backseat, slowly and carefully. There were two nurses waiting for us in the front hall of the hospital as we entered.

"We're going to operate right away," Dr. Toxie said.

I must have blacked out then for I remember little else that night, except when they gave me ether. I had had it once before when Dr. Toxie had taken out my tonsils and adenoids and found it not unpleasant. I remember distinctly the sensation of it taking over my consciousness, of not fighting it, and all the things going round and round in my head and not caring to stop them. I remembered nothing else after that until I began to awaken from the ether and saw I was in a strange bed in a strange room and I looked out a window near my bed and I could see a street that seemed strange to me, too, and houses that weren't on our street. And I felt someone looking at me and I realized it was my mother and beside her a young girl in a white nurse's uniform looking down at me, too. I thought I knew that girl from somewhere and then it came to me that it was Ruby Davis, who was in my class all through school and I thought, What is Ruby Davis doing in a nurse's uniform?

I looked away from her and over at Mother and I tried to smile at her. Mother whispered, "Hello, darling."

I closed my eyes and I was half-conscious then but when I heard the voice of my Great Aunt Loula, I opened my eyes to see if it really was her. I saw that it was and so I closed my eyes again and Aunt Loula was whispering in that loud, desperate way she had of whispering, saying she couldn't sleep at all last night, worrying about me. As soon as it was daylight she got dressed and without waking Doc decided to come over to the hospital to see if I had made it through the night.

I lost consciousness then for a moment and when I came to again, Mother and Aunt Loula were talking and I heard Aunt Loula say, "Daisy called to say he was going to be taken to the hospital, and then she called back and said they had begun the operation because his appendix had burst and she began to cry and bring up Mr. Billy Brooks dying of a ruptured appendix."

Aunt Loula stopped talking then and Mother walked over to the bed and looked at me and I heard her say, "He's coming out of the ether now. Just before you came up on the porch he opened his eyes and smiled at me."

"Bless his heart," Aunt Loula said.

"Will you stay with him for a second while I call Mama and Brother Hotchkiss? When I knew his appendix had burst I called Brother Hotchkiss and asked him to pray for him."

I heard Mother leave the room then and Aunt Loula got in the chair next to my bed and I opened my eyes and I was glad to see her, for I'd always loved her a lot and knew she loved me. "Yes," she said to me once, "I love anything with a drop of my families' blood," and then laughed with her own peculiar laugh.

I was in the hospital for ten days. Ruby Davis was my nurse and we talked about our time in high school and what had become of our friends and one afternoon she told me I was very lucky to be alive, that my appendix had burst and they thought I might die and that's why my mother had called Brother

Hotchkiss, the Methodist minister, to ask him to pray for me. She said after the operation, Dr. Toxie stayed in the room with me for over an hour to be sure I was going to live.

I asked Mother about what Ruby had told me and she said yes, it was true, but it was behind us now and she didn't want to talk about it. Then she began to cry and had to leave the room and I felt terrible seeing her cry and I called to her to please come back into the room. That afternoon my grandmother came to stay with me so my mother could get some rest and I was tired, but I couldn't get to sleep and I asked her if she would sing a hymn to me like she used to when I was little and she said she would and what hymn would I like to hear? I asked her to choose one and she sang, "Blessed Assurance," and then "Shall We Gather at the River," both favorites of mine and I went sound asleep.

The third day of my stay at the hospital I began to have lots of company. Aunt Loula, Aunt Lida, my cousin Nannie, and friends from town.

On the tenth day Dr. Toxie came to examine me and when he finished, asked me how would I like to go home. I said I would like it, although in truth I wasn't so anxious to go, as I was the only patient in the hospital and I was enjoying all the attention I was getting from my friends and family.

The next morning Nannie and my mother came to get me and I said good-bye to the three nurses and thanked them for all their kindness.

My mother insisted I get back in bed when I got home.

I had a letter from John Pelletti waiting for me, saying he was having a lazy summer and hoped I was having a good time in Texas and he would see me soon.

I wrote him back telling him about my operation and asked him to write me again and give me news of our friends.

Two days later Dr. Toxie told Mother she shouldn't be keeping me in bed, that it would help me to get my strength back to start walking around and that to let me eat whatever I wanted. Mother was obedient, and I dressed and got out of bed.

That night after supper I was visiting with my mother and father and my grandmother. We were sitting on the front porch and Daddy had brought me a letter from the school in Pasadena telling me of our new living arrangements. The school had rented two large houses, each having three floors and all students, except those living at home, would be housed there. The girls in one house, the boys in another. In the letter she told the price of rooms. The double rooms had to be shared and she said that John Forsht had asked to room with me and would I let her know if I would like that and the probable date of my arrival as soon as possible. I hadn't thought of leaving in all the excitement of the operation and the hospital, but I suddenly realized it was almost August and I would have to leave in a month.

"I tell you what I think," my grandmother said. "I don't think he should ride a bus back to California in this heat. He's still recovering from the operation and I think he should take the train. Even riding in the coach would be easier on him than riding in an old hot, dusty bus. Whatever the difference between the cost of a bus ticket and a coach train ticket is, I want to pay for it and please don't argue with me about this, Big Horton."

And for once he didn't and accepted her offer.

My cousin Nannie took me in her car to the train station on the day I was to leave. My mother rode in with us. There were no tearful farewells this time from my Grandmother Brooks before we drove off. All the way into Houston, Mother and Nannie discussed my grandmother's move. She had decided to rent the Wharton house temporarily until she was sure she didn't want to live again in Wharton. Nannie said everyone thought my mother and father should take over the house, but Mother said that wasn't to be.

The train was certainly more comfortable than the bus. I could walk around when I felt like it. There was a restroom to be used whenever I needed it, and food was available in the diner. The seats were comfortable and I was sure I would be able to sleep, but I couldn't. My mind kept skipping around, thinking first about Wharton and my grandmother and her leaving, and then about Pasadena and my friends and what school would be like the coming year.

Then, too, began the kind of inner dialogue I was to have so often with myself throughout the next few years. What if I couldn't get a job in the theater? (Movies never occurred to me.) Should I come back to the playhouse for the third year if I were asked? Could my parents afford that? Would they be willing? I remembered Jody Schwartzberg saying that if you want to be in the theater, get to New York. How do you get to New York, I thought, if you have no money and you have no prospects for a job? If you want to be in movies there's a chance in a thousand that a talent scout could see you in a show in Pasadena and offer you a contract or at least a part in a movie, but whoever heard of a scout coming all the way from Broadway to look for talent?

I remembered Jody Schwartzberg saying that there were thousands of young people coming into New York every year looking for work in the theater, and I said then, over and over to myself, why do you think out of those thousands you are going to be one of the lucky ones?

Then I remembered Mr. Brown saying in one of his lectures that it was too bad the motion pictures had killed off the stock companies because that was the best training ground for young actors. I remembered one of the students saying it was the Depression that had caused them to close and maybe when the Depression is over they will all open again. Mr. Brown answered that was wishful thinking, that the Depression didn't help, but they were doomed anyway. That the stock companies were killed by motion pictures just like they killed vaudeville, and they will never be revived, not in that form anyway. And then someone asked did he think it will finally kill all theaters? And he said, no, he didn't think that, he thought the theater would survive. Maybe not as we knew it today, but in some form.

I remembered John Forsht asking him if he thought it was possible for a young person to make a living in the theater in New York and his answering that is was possible, anything was possible, but it is getting more difficult all the time. I remembered, too, his saying, "Why do you young people always want to go to New York? I never went to New York, I played in stock companies certainly, but I never went to New York and look what I have done, established a theater, and I produce and direct plays and I make a living. I'm not a rich man, but I make an honest, honorable living and do the kind of plays I can be proud of."

Maybe I thought then I shouldn't go to New York, either, maybe I should look around and start a theater of my own someplace. Where? In Wharton, Texas? Where? How? How old was Mr. Brown when he started the playhouse? How old is he now?

Jody Schwartzberg said the playhouse was always needing money and depended on the gifts of rich people to keep going.

On and on through the night in my mind I wrote scenarios for my future. Some were triumphant and some were depressing and ended badly. I tried to shut all these thoughts off so I could get to sleep, but I couldn't. Fear and anxiety had hold of me and they wouldn't turn me loose. Finally, I dozed off around seven in the morning, but I was awakened by the voice of a cheerful conductor around eight, calling out some town or other. I gave up then and went to wash my face and forgot about sleeping.

CHAPTER 6

Rosamond Pinchot

Aunt Mag and Uncle Walt met me at the train station and took me directly to the playhouse office. This time they made no mention of Thanksgiving or Christmas. Aunt Mag was all exercised about my grandmother's move to Houston and had hoped she would settle in California. She kept saying over and over, "I bet she'll end up here someday."

They let me off at the playhouse school office and I thanked them and kissed Aunt Mag good-bye and promised to keep in touch. I looked over at the playhouse before going into the office, and nothing had changed. I hoped I would see someone I knew, but didn't, so I took my suitcase and went on into the office.

The girl at the desk was new, but I told her my name and asked if Mrs. Walkup was in. She said she was and rang her on the phone and told her I was there and Mrs. Walkup said to send me in right away.

Mrs. Walkup was waiting by the door when I went into her office. She asked about my summer and I told her of my appendicitis and that it had been difficult, but I was fine now and I was glad to be back.

"I think you're going to be pleased with the house you boys will live in," she said. "John Forsht is already settled in and is expecting you today. It just occurred to me he might be working over at the playhouse office right this minute. Let me find out."

She went to the door then and asked the secretary to call over to the office to see if John Forsht was there and if he was, have him come over here.

When she came back into the room she went to her desk and looked through some papers.

"I've written down somewhere the name of the play you'll be doing first. Let's see. Oh, here, I think this is it. Oh, yes. *The Importance of Being Earnest,* by Oscar Wilde. Do you know it?"

"Yes, I do," I said.

"Do you like it?"

"Yes, I do. I certainly do."

"Miss Janet Scott is to direct all the plays you seniors do this year. How does it feel to be called a senior?"

"Fine, I guess."

There was a knock on the door and Mrs. Walkup called out, "Come in," and the door opened and there was John Forsht. I went over to him and we shook hands.

"John, tell him how much you like the place you're living in."

"It's nice," John said, not sounding as enthusiastic as Mrs. Walkup.

"Can you walk Horton over to the house and show him your room?" she asked.

"Sure."

My suitcase was in the outer office and I picked it up on our way out.

"How far is the house?" I asked.

"Three blocks."

We were out on the street by now and I saw several people sitting in the playhouse courtyard, but no one I recognized.

"We go this way," John said, pointing right.

"Is the house as nice as she says it is?"

"It's all right. Kind of rundown but comfortable. It's huge. Three stories. We are on the second floor."

"Are any of our class in the house?"

"Not too many," he said. "Pelletti as you know lives at home and so does Jack Lescoulie and Peter Engel. Ralph Clanton and Bob de Sylva are there. Charles Robinson hasn't come back yet. I think he's supposed to. There it is," he said, pointing to our house.

It did seem gigantic, and not well kept. It was shingled and the shingles had not weathered well, a few needed replacing.

"It looks better inside," John Forsht said.

We went up the porch stairs to the front door of the house. John opened the door and we went inside to a huge front hall where four boys were talking, none of them I knew or had ever seen before. John didn't speak to them nor did they speak to him.

Our room was just off the left of the staircase and it was also large, with two single beds, a straight chair and a rocking chair, a table with a table lamp, and four large curtainless windows, but with shades that could be pulled down.

"Well," John said. "This is it. Not fancy, but okay. The beds are comfortable enough."

"Is there a closet?"

"Sure." He opened a door in the center of the room and I saw a closet that would certainly accommodate the few clothes I had.

"Come on. I want to show you something," John said, going out to the hallway, and I followed him. He went down two doors, and knocked on the door; when there was no answer he opened the door.

"I want you to see how a lot of the new guys live."

The room was about as large as ours, but had only a single bed. There was a handsome rug on the floor, and equally attractive curtains on the windows and a bedspread that matched the curtains.

"How do you like that?" John Forsht asked me.

Just then a mild-looking man wearing a tweed jacket and corduroy pants and smoking a pipe looked into the room.

"What are you doing in here?" he said, laughing.

"Just snooping around," John Forsht said. "Showing Horton how the rich live. Horton, this is Doc Granby."

"Hello," he said as we shook hands.

"He's a Princeton graduate," John Forsht said.

"Don't hold that against me," he said, laughing. "Come see my room."

He started out to the hall and John and I followed him. His room was fairly small and at the end of the hall. It, too, had curtains, a rug on the floor, and a bedspread. There were two bookcases filled with books, and a typewriter and drawing materials on his desk.

I went over to the bookcase and looked at his books.

"Do you like to read?" he asked.

"I sure do. You have a lot of books. I have a lot at home, but it never occurred to me to bring them."

"Cost me a fortune," he said. "But I need to have them around. You can borrow any of them you like. Whenever you like."

"How's Pelletti?" I asked John.

"He's good."

"Did Margi Skouras come back?"

"Yes."

"I bet that makes him happy?"

"It does."

"Did Mary Virginia Palmer come back?"

"Yes."

"Charlotte Sturges didn't."

"I heard that."

"I knew that last spring. She told me then she wasn't coming back. She's gone to Germany to study dancing with Mary Wigman."

"Is that so? I'd love to go to Germany. I'd love to see Alexander Moissi's *Hamlet.* Just once."

I went often to Doc Granby's room and read his books and magazines. It was there that I saw *Theater Arts* edited by Edith Isaacs for the first time and I was fascinated by it and spent all my spare time reading it. It was there, too, I think I first read an article on Eleonora Duse by Stark Young, and found he was also a theater critic for *The New Republic,* a magazine Doc also subscribed to.

* * *

The second-year students were given a small theater over the patio restaurant. The plays were to be rehearsed for three weeks and performed for one matinee and two evening performances. Students were to design and build the sets, work backstage, stage manage, act in the plays, and one student would assist our director, Miss Scott, for each play. There was no admission charged and how large an audience attended was up to us, as Mr. Brown said he wanted us to have the experience of being in complete charge of managing a theater, including finding an audience.

Janet Scott, our director, announced at our first meeting the casting of *The Importance of Being Earnest*. I was to be Ernest; John Forsht, Algernon; Peggy Carter, Cecily; and Jody Schwartzberg, Lady Bracknell.

I went to Miss Townsend the next morning with a copy of the play. She asked if I would like to try for an English accent and I said I would, so she had me read a few of Ernest's lines from his first scene with his friend Algernon. Algernon began the scene and she read his lines, "How are you, my dear Ernest. What brings you to town," in her most clipped, brusque manner.

I was so fascinated by her reading and her accent that I forgot to respond with my line, "Oh, pleasure, pleasure! What else should bring one anywhere? Eating as usual, I see, Algy." When I did respond, she stopped me on the second pleasure, and repeated it for me several times and asked me then to repeat it, which I did, but not to her satisfaction and she wrote it out for me phonetically and I tried again. This time with a little more success. Then she decided to make a list phonetically of all the vowel sounds as an Englishman of a certain class would pronounce them. We spent at least half an hour on that, and then she asked that I write out the whole part phonetically, reminding me to write the vowel sounds as we had rehearsed them.

The next day, when we were reading the play for Miss Scott, I tried remembering all Miss Townsend had told me, and John, as Algernon, was reading with what I assumed was his idea of an English accent, for I had never heard him speak so before, and Mary Virginia playing Gwendolyn spoke just as she always did and I waited for Miss Scott to stop her and say where is the accent, but she didn't. Then Jody Schwartzberg began as Lady Bracknell: "Mr. Worthing. Rise, sir, from this semi-incumbent posture. It is most indecorous," blaring out the words so loudly that I thought she sounded more like the widow in *Liliom,* and with her idea of an English accent. When she got to Lady Bracknell's speech beginning, "Pardon me, you are not engaged to anyone. When you do become engaged to someone, I, or your father, should his health permit him, will inform you of the fact," Miss Scott interrupted her. "Is that an English accent you're attempting?"

"Yes, ma'am," Jody said.

"And you Horton and John?"

"Yes, ma'am," we both said.

"Well, let's forget the accent. There is no time really for that."

"But I want to have an English accent," Jody said. "I mean she has to have an accent, doesn't she? Otherwise she won't be real. She will just be me."

"I'm sure you feel that, dear," Miss Scott said not unkindly. "But I'm your director. Just speak naturally for me and later, much later, we might try for an accent. This goes for you, too, Horton and John. Now begin again, Jody, please."

Jody began again but on her third line stopped.

"It sounds so flat and uninteresting. I don't think I have any character now at all."

And so it went, Jody stopping on every third line to complain about how dull it sounded, until finally Miss Scott said quite sharply, "Jody. Believe me. I have asked you to give up nothing. You had no English accent, only a phony caricature of an English accent. Now I am the director, and you will do as I say or I will have to replace you." That shut Jody up and we proceeded with no more interruptions.

We read though the play for two days and then Miss Scott had us on our feet, still reading from our scripts, and began the staging. After the second day of that she said, "I want you all off the book by the end of the week." I went home that night and started memorizing.

After three weeks of rehearsal we did the play for three performances in our little theater. We had a full dress rehearsal the afternoon of our first performance with lights, props, and in our costumes, and without English accents. For the actual performance our audience consisted of our classmates and a few relatives and friends. I have no idea what those performances were like. Miss Scott had mostly worried about the staging and whether we could be heard. Except for her insisting that we not try English accents, she was kind and supportive. I got laughs on some of my lines, which had never happened to me before and which at first startled me, but when they continued, I realized they were not laughing at me, but at what I was doing as the character. The next performance, a matinee, they didn't laugh as much, but that night they laughed again and sometimes in different places. I asked Miss Scott about that and she said different audiences always reacted differently and that when she was acting she grew to expect that, but some actresses she knew would analyze what they were doing when they got a laugh, and would try to repeat what they thought got the laugh, whether it was a certain reading of a line or a piece of stage business. She said when she tried doing that it just made her self-conscious and her acting became flat and stilted.

On one of her trips to New York, Jody Schwartzberg had seen Francis Lederer, a popular star from Europe in his New York play, *Autumn Crocus*. She had been very taken with him and managed to go backstage and meet him, and they had kept up a correspondence ever since. He had written her recently that he was coming to the West Coast to do a film and she was ecstatic. After he arrived he invited her to his home for lunch. She no longer talked of Eva Le Gallienne or the Civic Repertory Theater. Everything now was Francis Lederer.

Elisabeth Bergner, the famous German actress, also was now in films and two of them, *Escape Me Never* and *As You Like It,* were very popular in America. I had never seen Francis Lederer perform but I had seen both of Elisabeth Bergner's films and I, along with most of the other students, was very taken with her. She had a definite style of acting and many of the girls in our class began to imitate her mannerisms. Jody Schwartzberg said Francis Lederer knew Elisabeth Bergner and thought she was a great actress and also thought that most American acting was flat and one-dimensional beside German acting.

John Forsht said he always knew German acting was the best and that Alexander Moissi was the greatest actor in the world today. I wished often I was German like John Forsht and could perhaps one day be a great German actor like Moissi. Francis Lederer was not a great actor, John Forsht insisted, but a personality. Jody Schwartzberg heard him say that once and they got into a bitter argument.

One day two men appeared in the playhouse patio, sitting in the sun, smoking cigarettes. They looked very European and had a certain air of mystery about them. One was a small, dark man, very boyish with sad eyes, and quite handsome. The other was a tall, lean man, with a beaklike nose and hair that stood straight up, which he kept closely cropped.

Jody Schwartzberg heard them talking one morning in the patio, and, realizing they were German, went up to them in her brazen way, and introduced herself as a friend of Francis Lederer. From then on every time they were in the patio for even five minutes, Jody Schwartzberg, it seemed, would be talking to them. I was curious about them and I asked her why they were in Pasadena.

"They are here to do a play," she said. "They start rehearsals next week."

"What's the play?" I asked.

"A dramatization of *The Brothers Karamazov,* by Dostoyevsky. Do you know the novel?"

"No, I don't."

"They say its just tremendous. The novel, that is. They doubt if it can ever really be dramatized, but their characters are so challenging they decided to do it. They're from Max Reinhardt's theater. They've acted with Elisabeth Bergner and are devoted friends of Francis Lederer. I asked Francis about them and he says they are both extremely talented. Guess who they're living with now until they start rehearsals here next week?"

"Who?"

"Marlene Dietrich. She's very kind, they say."

"Is she from Reinhardt, too?"

"No, I don't think so. They had to leave Germany because of politics. They hope this play will help establish them in America. I don't think they have much money."

"How do you know that?"

"Francis Lederer told me. The small, dark fellow is Martin Koslick and the other is Hans von Twardowski."

John Pelletti, John Forsht, and I went to *The Brothers Karamazov* together. I had wanted to read the novel first and Doc Granby had a copy in his room and loaned it to me, but I had only gotten a third of the way through by the time I saw the play. John Forsht had read it in college and he said it was a great novel but he wondered, because of its length and complexity, if it could ever be successfully dramatized.

The play was in many scenes and Gilmor Brown had given it a handsome production. Martin Koslick played Aliocha the youngest Karamazov, and Hans von Twardowski played Smerdyakov.

The rest of the cast were Americans and all adequate, but Koslick and Twardowski were mesmerizing. They seemed to be doing really very little, but with such concentration and quiet authority that you really watched no one else and couldn't wait for them to come back onstage.

At intermission I asked Jody Schwartzberg how old Martin Koslick was.

"How old do you think?" she asked.

"Well, his character is twenty-two years old," I said.

"Well, he's not twenty-two years old. I can tell you that. Who do you think is the oldest, Martin or Hans?"

"Hans?"

"No, Martin is several years older."

"How do you know?"

"Francis Lederer told me. Dietrich is coming to see them next week they say, and they've promised to introduce me to her."

I was so taken with Koslick and Twardowski that I went to see two more performances. I was there the night Marlene Dietrich was supposed to attend. Jody Schwartzberg was there that night, too, but Dietrich didn't show up.

Going home that night after the performance I thought of Charlotte Sturges in Germany and wondered how she was and what it would be like to be in Germany and studying acting and maybe one day being part of Max Reinhardt's company. I didn't know then, of course, I would one day be in *The Eternal Road,* directed by Max Reinhardt and choreographed by Benjamin Zemach.

I asked Jody Schwartzberg to ask Koslick and Twardowski if they knew Alexander Moissi and had they seen him play Hamlet. She did, but said they thought his day had past. I didn't tell John Forsht that. He had now been given a record of Moissi doing scenes from *Hamlet* and he played it over and over on Doc Granby's record player. I listened to it once, but not knowing any German found it difficult to follow.

Two weeks after Christmas vacation we were told after breakfast not to leave the dining room as Mrs. Walkup wanted to talk to us. In about fifteen minutes she came in all smiles and said, "Good morning" in a most cheerful way and asked if everyone were present and when no one answered she began to count and said she believed everyone was. Again, she smiled and looking all around the room at each of us said, "Now, I don't want any of you to be alarmed, but there has been a case of polio, a slight case mind you, of one of the boys living here, and to be on the safe side the Board of Health has asked that each of you be given a shot and that you be quarantined here for at least two weeks. Again, I assure you there is nothing, absolutely nothing, to be alarmed about, but we feel we have to comply with the authorities."

"What about classes?" one of the first-year boys called out.

Mrs. Walkup said classes would be suspended and that the boys in the second-year class could be taken to the doctor first. When Doc Granby heard that, he raised his hand and asked Mrs. Walkup, "May I go over with John and Horton? We're friends."

"I don't see why not," she said, still smiling.

"When are we going?" Ralph Clanton asked.

"Right now, darling," she said. "We have cars waiting."

We followed Mrs. Walkup out the door then and got in her car. I sat in the front with her and John and Doc got in the back.

When we arrived, the doctor's office was empty except for a nurse. She was as smiling and cheerful as Mrs. Walkup and seemed to be expecting us. "Good morning," the nurse said.

"Good morning, nurse," Mrs. Walkup said. "We are here for the shots."

"Oh, yes, the doctor is expecting you," the nurse said.

She picked up the phone and announced to the doctor or someone that we were there and she put the phone down and said to Mrs. Walkup, "Who's first?"

Mrs. Walkup looked at the three of us. "Any volunteers?" she asked.

I don't know what got into me, but I found myself saying, "I'll go first."

"That's a brave boy," Mrs. Walkup said. "Come on. I'll go with you."

The doctor and another nurse were waiting for us in his office. Mrs. Walkup introduced me and he told me to roll up my right sleeve, which I did. Mrs. Walkup came next to me and took my hand and smiled at me.

"It will be over soon," she said and continued smiling in that confident way she had been doing ever since she had come into the dining room that morning.

The doctor came over to me then with his needle and I closed my eyes so I wouldn't see what he was going to do, and I felt Mrs. Walkup squeeze my hand and I felt the needle go in then and I gave a little gasp and Mrs. Walkup squeezed my hand again and she said, "You can open your eyes, Horton, it's all over."

On the third day of quarantine, Eric, from the third-year group, came up to me and said he and another fellow in the third year had gotten permission to rehearse and do a showing of *The Emperor Jones* while we were in quarantine, and that Miss Scott had agreed to direct. She had suggested he approach me to stage-manage as she felt I was very reliable. Would I be interested? I said I was and that afternoon Miss Scott came to the house and we began.

I had never seen a production of a Eugene O'Neill play, although in Wharton I had bought and read *Mourning Becomes Electra* and *Beyond the Horizon*.

Miss Scott talked that first day about O'Neill and his place in the American theater. She told about his one-act plays often dealing with the sea, his experiences as a sailor, and of his first productions in New York by the Provincetown Players at the Provincetown Playhouse. She had not seen any of those productions, but she had seen *Anna Christie, The Great God Brown,* and *Strange Interlude.*

She talked of Lynn Fontanne in *Strange Interlude,* but the actress that had impressed her most was Pauline Lord in *Anna Christie.* She said, in her opinion, Miss Lord was our greatest actress, and she would never forget the power of her performance. She had seen her, too, in *They Knew What They Wanted,* and said she was equally fine in that, and was now appearing in New York in *The Late Christopher Bean,* which she hadn't seen. "Anyway, that's enough about that. Let's get to the play."

After rehearsals I took the copy of *The Emperor Jones* Miss Scott had given me and read it through. I was puzzled why Eric had chosen to perform a play about a forty-year-old black American. Eric was twenty-five at the most, from somewhere in the Midwest, white, with a pronounced midwestern accent, but then I thought of Lee Cobb, twenty-five, playing King Herod so powerfully.

The play was given the afternoon of the day before quarantine ended. Eric was no Lee Cobb and afterward the first-year students were harsh and rude in their comments. Doc Granby, always kind, said he thought it was courageous of them to attempt it at all under such conditions.

That night in our room, John Forsht did Hamlet's soliloquy beginning, "O, what a rogue and peasant slave am I!" in German for Doc and me. We were very impressed, and Doc said, "I don't think Moissi could be any better," which of course pleased John a great deal.

In the spring we were in rehearsal with a Spanish play about a young girl about to become a nun, who falls in love with a soldier. The soldier was the only role for a man in the play and it was double-cast with John Forsht playing one performance and John Pelletti the next. I was the stage manager and also helped with the building of the sets at night after rehearsals. I worked the night of my birthday until four, and would have stayed on until rehearsal next morning, as we had gotten behind in our set construction and the dress rehearsal was only two days away, but when my coworkers heard it was my birthday they insisted I go home. The scene shop was in a rundown section of Pasadena and as I walked home that night, the streets deserted, no moon, no stars, I began to wonder again what I would do when I graduated from the playhouse in May. Should I go back there for another year if I was invited back? Should I try to go to New York like Jody Schwartzberg and some others planned to do? John Forsht said he was determined to get to New York some way. Pelletti was not going to New York but was staying here, hoping as he said, to get a part in a play on the main stage of the playhouse and be discovered by some studio scout.

Several months earlier I had gone to see a play about John Brown and I had been very taken with the actress playing the wife of the oldest Brown son. I had never seen or heard of her before, but I thought she was beautiful and had great stage presence.

Jody Schwartzberg was there that night with Robert de Sylva and during intermission she told us that the actress Rosamond Pinchot was a New York socialite. She had been discovered on a boat going to or from Europe, Jody wasn't sure which, by Max Reinhardt, and had been cast at eighteen in his production of *The Miracle.* Her beauty had impressed everyone and she became an overnight sensation. I asked how she knew all that and she said Martin Koslick and Hans von Twardowski had told her. She said she had come here to do a play away from New York to get some acting experience.

"She obviously," Jody said with great authority, "is not much of an actress and needs a great deal of training."

I didn't agree and told her so.

"Well," Jody said in that imperious way of hers, "you're just dazzled by her beauty."

"No, not just that," I argued. "I find something very touching and vulnerable about her."

"Vulnerable, indeed," Jody said. "That's just sheer panic, because she doesn't know what she's doing. Anyway, I don't feel too sorry for her. Her family are very, very rich."

"They are?"

"Oh, yes. Very, very, very rich. Her uncle is governor of Pennsylvania."

After the performance I decided to go backstage and speak to Rosamond Pinchot, and tell her how much I liked her in the play. Her dressing room was in the basement of the playhouse and she was alone and still in her costume when I got there. She seemed pleased that I had come back and asked if I would wait out in the hall until she changed her clothes and we could talk a little. I said

I'd be happy to, and I waited in the hall patiently until she came out. And she was a beauty. Tall, taller than I was by several inches, even wearing shoes with no heels, broad shouldered, tanned, her blond hair worn shoulder length. She asked if I would like to visit for a while in the patio, as she felt by this time the audience had all gone. She said she would have ordinarily invited me to the restaurant for a drink, but was tired and could visit only for a few minutes. The patio was empty when we got there. We sat down and she asked me about my reaction to the play, and told me she was doing it because, as Jody had said, she needed experience. She then told me about being discovered by Max Reinhardt, and being cast in *The Miracle*. She asked why I was in Pasadena and I told her I was in school and was about to graduate. I began asking her about Reinhardt and she said he was a genius and he had found a way to make whatever she did, onstage, interesting and theatrical. Now that she was away from him and on her own she felt very insecure and realized more and more how little she knew. I said I didn't sense that at all when I saw her perform. I felt she knew exactly what she was doing. She was pleased to hear that, of course, and asked what I wanted to do when I finished school. I said I wanted somehow to get to New York and find a job in the theater.

"That's what you should do," she said. "That's the only place to be if you want to be an actor. I'll go back as soon as I finish here unless I get a job in pictures, which I don't want to do particularly, but I have an offer and it would be experience. What I really want to do is another play, although I don't think I'm ready to do a play in New York just yet. I think I should study first. There's a wonderful teacher in New York, I hear. Maria Ouspenskaya. Did you ever hear of her?"

"No," I said.

"She was with the Moscow Art Theater and teaches now in New York. I think I'll study with her when I get back."

We met often after that during the run of her play. We would talk about New York and the theater there and Reinhardt and the European theater that she had seen.

I remembered all this that night, walking home from the scene shop. I remembered, too, she had given me her address in New York, and I thought I might write her and ask her advice about coming to New York, but I never did.

I had been neglecting my lessons with Miss Townsend because of my stage-managing duties and the scenery building, but I started as soon as the play was over. She had me again on "My Last Duchess," and insisted I memorize the whole poem. She said it was quite a dramatic poem and I would learn much by working on it once more. After I had finished my lesson, Miss Townsend lit a cigarette and offered me one.

"Miss Townsend," I said. "May I ask you a question?"

"Yes, Horton. What is it? You look so serious. Is something wrong?"

"No," I said, "not really, it's just something I'm not sure about what to do. I mean whether I should even consider it."

"What's that?" she asked.

"Do you think I'm foolish to even consider going to New York when I finish here? Do you think I could find a place in the New York theater?"

"Anything is possible, Horton. It would depend I would think on your determination. Louise tried it for three or four months and she couldn't take the rejection and left. By the way," she continued, "I spoke to Louise last night and it occurred to me since you have become very proficient in phonetics you should travel around Texas and write down phonetically the different dialects. It would be great training for your ear and in the end might be a way to make some money. There is a need for this kind of research."

"I'll certainly think about it," I said, my heart sinking, sure this was her way of telling me not to consider at all a career as an actor, and to stay away from New York.

"By the way," she said, "what are you doing for the summer?"

"I have no plans right now," I said. "I'll go home for a while and then I don't know."

"I teach in the summer at Martha's Vineyard," she said. "And it's lovely there. Louise and I rent a cottage for the summer. There's a stock company there, too, called the Rice Playhouse. The whole thing is owned and managed by two old and dear friends of mine, Phidela and Betty Rice. They're lovely people. Unfortunately only girls seem to be able to pay to come to their school, so Mr. and Mrs. Rice make it possible for me to ask three or four boys each summer to come and study with me and work with the girls on scenes and in plays. They pay very little. You get room and board, of course, and the food is very good, I might add. Also a small stipend of five dollars a week to keep you in cigarettes and toiletries, and from time to time a part will come up in the stock company that you might be right for. We've already asked Joseph Anthony this year if he would be interested and he has accepted. Louise saw your friends John Forsht and John Pelletti in their plays last week and I'm thinking of asking them and I wondered if you would be interested . You don't have to give me your answer right now, but I would like to know before the week is out."

"I can give you my answer now," I said. "I want to go."

"Splendid," she said. "Splendid."

I couldn't wait to get back to the playhouse and to find John Forsht and John Pelletti and tell them the news. John Forsht was as delighted as I was, but Pelletti said he wasn't going to ever leave California.

I wrote my parents that night a long letter telling them of Miss Townsend's offer to me and John Forsht and how much it meant to me. I said I hated asking for any more help, but would they consider paying my way to Martha's Vineyard, but if they couldn't afford it at this time I would understand, and would I then have their permission to write my grandmother and ask if she would give me the fare. I reassured them I would be on my own once I got to the island, because I would be given furnished room and board and paid five dollars a week. I also explained that I would have been willing to work while I was in Wharton to earn the money for the train fare, but my schedule would only permit my being in Wharton a week before leaving for Massachusetts. I asked, too, for permission to bring John Forsht home with me as we would be making the trip to Martha's Vineyard together.

Five days later I got a letter from my mother. She began her letter as she always did, "Dearest Son." Then she went on to say how proud she was of me and thought being asked to Martha's Vineyard by Miss Townsend a great honor and a sure sign of her belief in my talent. She said she and my daddy would certainly welcome John Forsht or any of my friends at any time. The next day I got a letter from my father, only the second he had written me since I had been in Pasadena. His began "My Darling Boy," and he went on to say he was proud of me and was sure I would become a great success in my chosen field, and he would at this time be able to scrape up the money to get me to Martha's Vineyard, but I must realize that times were very hard in Wharton, that in spite of all of Roosevelt's hard work, the Depression was still on, and cotton bringing in hardly anything, the poor devils who were farmers were barely getting by. So, that from here on, I must understand he couldn't be counted on for anything else. He also said he would welcome at any time any friends of mine and he looked forward to meeting John Forsht.

John and I were both impressed that Joseph Anthony had been asked, and had accepted to go to Martha's Vineyard, as we knew that Mr. Brown considered him a fine actor, with a very promising future. He had already appeared professionally with Helen Gahagan Douglas in *Mary Queen of Scots* for quite a run at a Los Angeles theater and had been in a number of plays on the main stage at the playhouse, where I had seen him do the Dauphin in *Saint Joan.* He was rarely around the playhouse these days, because he was acting with the third-year students in the Padua Hills Theater.

I had come across two books by Stark Young, *The Flower in Drama* and *Glamour,* in Doc's room. In one of his essays on acting I found this:

The German Theater is admirable first of all for its sense of ensemble, its reverence for the whole effect. German acting,

more over, does the folk thing well, the obstinacy of revolutionary motives, the vagaries of ordinary comedy. It has
audacity too, and this—though often unregulated by a finely
civilized and urbane relaxation and choice—has given it a certain lead in the morbid and the bold ventures into new fields.
German acting renders profoundly the turgid deep soul.

I copied this and showed it to John Forsht and it pleased him. I
was also interested in a series of imagined letters from dead actors
that Stark had written. There was a letter from Rachel, the legendary French actress, to Pauline Lord, David Garrick to John
Barrymore, and La Corrillana to Doris Keane. I knew by now
who Pauline Lord, Rachel, David Garrick, and John Barrymore
were, but I'd never heard of La Corrillana or Doris Keane. John
Forsht didn't know who they were, either, and Doc Granby had
never heard of La Corrillana, but he did know of Doris Keane. He
didn't know, though, if she was acting any longer, but said she
had some great successes on Broadway, including *The Czarina*
and *Romance,* which had been written by Edward Sheldon.
Edward Sheldon, he said, had written many popular plays for
Katharine Cornell and Lenore Ulric among others, and had been
struck by a mysterious illness at the height of his career which
left him blind, totally paralyzed, and unable to write.

Some years later, after I was a playwright, Agnes de Mille
spoke to me about Edward Sheldon. Ned Sheldon, she called
him. She said he was still alive, and she visited him often and
read to him. She said a number of the theater's leading actresses,
including Helen Hayes and Katharine Cornell, went regularly to
visit and read to him. She said he was very interested in young
writers and that she had spoken to him about me and my work

and he was eager to meet me. She said if I went I would never forget the visit, and urged me to go. I agreed and she arranged a meeting on a Friday at two o'clock and felt I should go alone. I was very nervous about the meeting, wondering what I should say, what he would be like, and how I would react.

He lived in the East Eighties, although whether in an apartment or in his own house I can't remember, nor do I remember who greeted me at the door when I rang the bell, whether a man or a woman, but I remember whoever it was saying they were Mr. Sheldon's secretary and that he was expecting me. I remember vividly being led into the living room, spacious and handsome, and before I had a chance to look around the room, hearing a voice saying, "Good afternoon, Mr. Foote," and I looked in the direction of the voice and there at the far end of the room, a man lying flat on a high, narrow bed, fully clothed, a black satin mask over his eyes, and the voice continued, "Won't you come closer. How good of you to come."

"Thank you," I said as I walked toward him.

"Agnes de Mille has told me a great deal about you and I'm so interested in all you're doing," he said as I approached him.

And so it went. I sat near him in a chair. He was handsomely dressed, and though he never moved he seemed in no pain. He asked me many questions about my writing, where I had come from and how I'd met Agnes.

I said I regretted never having seen any of his plays. I said I had read what Stark Young had written about Doris Keane in *Romance,* and it must have been an extraordinary performance. He said it was and I asked him if she was his favorite actress, and he smiled, I remember, and paused and said, "She's certainly one of them, and she is a very, very great actress."

Then he again began asking me questions about my plays, and he wanted to know if I'd seen Agnes dance. I said many times, and he said he regretted that he never had, and I wanted to ask him about writing and did he prefer collaborating or writing by himself, but I felt shy and didn't. Then he asked me if I wanted something to drink or a cigarette and I thanked him and said I didn't.

I had been told by Agnes not to stay more than a half hour for fear of tiring him, so I glanced at my watch and saw my time was up and I rose and said I would have to be going now. He thanked me for coming and hoped I would come again and perhaps stay longer next time.

Besides reading about Doris Keane in *The Flower in Drama*, I'd also read what Stark Young had to say about Duse and Bernhardt, and it seemed terrible to me that I would never now get to see them perform.

Many years later when I became friends with Stark Young, I told him about my meeting with Edward Sheldon and I asked him about Duse and Bernhardt and the differences in their techniques. He said Duse moved him as no other actress had, but he also had great admiration for Bernhardt and her technique. He said he felt Bernard Shaw's famous comparison between the two really meant very little except indicating how Duse affected the emotion of her admirers and how little interest Shaw had in the frankly theatrical art of Bernhardt. Stark said he responded to many different approaches to acting and theater and felt it was limiting to insist on only one approach.

I used to listen to Stark by the hour as he talked of the actors he had seen. He was a great champion of John Gielgud and thought

Laurence Olivier's *Oedipus Rex* mediocre. I had seen Olivier's production of *Oedipus* and I was profoundly moved by the play and his performances, but I didn't argue with Stark for fear I would seem provincial and ignorant, since he had seen many productions of the play. Indeed the only real disagreement I had with him ever was over Katherine Anne Porter, a great favorite of mine, whom he dismissed one day as a writer. Later I was told by Wales Bowman, his friend and companion for many years, not to take what he said about Miss Porter seriously, that he was hurt when she said publicly that she didn't like his novel *So Red the Rose*. Later, Stark told me, too, that he was hurt because she said *So Red the Rose* was vulgar and, since it was based on his family, it was like having your family that you loved called vulgar.

The day arrived for John and me to leave Pasadena for Texas. We were to take the interurban to the Los Angeles railroad station. It was then, as we were waiting for the interurban, that I realized fully I was leaving Pasadena and the playhouse, and that I might never see it again.

"John," I said, "do you realize we may never see Pasadena or the playhouse again, or any of our friends?"

"Yes, I've thought of that, but then I bet we will see it again someday."

It was forty years before I did and then only the outside. I had come to Pasadena to attend rehearsals of the musical version of *Gone With the Wind,* for which I had done the book. We were rehearsing night and day at the theater in the Pasadena Civic Center. I slipped off from rehearsals one night and went over to the playhouse. Mr. Brown had been dead many years by then and the school was no more. The theater building was shabby and neglected and plays hadn't been done there for some time. I thought of all the hopes and dreams of Mr. Brown and it saddened me that his theater was no longer being used as he wanted it to be.

But on this late spring day in 1935, I soon got over any feelings of sadness about leaving Pasadena or the playhouse and began to think of showing John Forsht around Wharton, wondering what Martha's Vineyard would be like, and how I was going to get from there to New York City and find acting jobs.

PART II

New York City

CHAPTER 7

Pauline Lord

I was in Martha's Vineyard for almost two months. Miss Townsend had me work on scenes from *Candida* with a number of her students. Near the end of the summer she directed John Forsht, a girl student from Virginia, and me in *The No 'Count Boy* by Paul Green, a three-character play about North Carolina rural blacks. It is an homage, at least in spirit, to Synge's *The Playboy of the Western World.* We performed this on the stage of the Rice Playhouse before a packed house.

It seems very strange to me now that she chose this play to do with three white actors, although at the time it didn't seem strange at all since the life in the play was much more familiar to me than the world of Marchbanks. I was cast as the No 'Count Boy and played him in blackface, and felt a freedom in my work on the part that I had never felt while working on the Shaw character. The actors from the stock company were in the audience as were people from the town. Few of the latter I'm sure had ever seen a black, much less a southern black, and they were very taken with the production.

During the summer John Forsht and I had become close friends with Joe Anthony, and we decided we would share an apartment in New York. Joe had a friend, Elizabeth Cope, who had been in his class at Pasadena and was now studying at Martha's Vineyard. She was wealthy, kind, and generous, and when she heard we were going to New York she offered to pay a first month's rent on an apartment she knew of on Sullivan Street in the Village, and nice it was, too, but when we heard the amount of the rent we realized it was more than we could afford and began to look for a cheaper place, which we found on MacDougal Street across from the Provincetown Playhouse.

John and I had taken a boat from Martha's Vineyard to New York City and Joe had come with Elizabeth Cope in her car. Earlier in the summer, just before leaving home, my father had given me fifty dollars to get started in New York with the warning that that was the very last money he would give me and never to ask for more. John had seven dollars as I remember and Joe had little more.

Fortunately we found jobs fairly soon: John and I working backstage for a musical called *The Provincetown Follies* at the Provincetown Playhouse. Joe, being a member of Equity, was able to get on Federal Theater and was soon cast in a play with Estelle Winwood, a leading New York actress.

On our first day in New York, John and I explored the subway. Unlike for my cousin Nannie, it had no terror at all for me, and we went immediately to the theater district to look around. We had received instructions from the actors in the Rice Stock Company on how to look for acting jobs, and we were eager to get started, but we could do very little while *The Provincetown Follies* was in rehearsal.

The apartment we found at MacDougal Street was in a tenement building. It had two very large rooms, a smaller room, and a separate kitchen. It was furnished with beds that were old but comfortable enough, a sofa and some chairs, all also very old. The kitchen was equipped after a fashion—a few dishes, some knives, forks, and spoons, a few pans, and a coffee pot. I had never cooked in my life, nor had John. Joe, efficient in all things, had some knowledge of cooking and the first week or so cooked for all of us, but when his Federal Theater rehearsals began, he had to stop and John and I were left to our own devices.

We soon found a drugstore at the corner of Eighth Street and Sixth Avenue that served a cheap breakfast. We ate our lunch in a drugstore uptown, for we had, as soon as the revue opened, begun taking the subway every weekday morning to Forty-second Street to look for acting jobs. We would start our search usually at the Empire Theater Building on Thirty-ninth Street across from the old Metropolitan Opera House, where there was at least one producer's office on each floor.

The tour of the Empire offices took about half an hour and then we would proceed up Broadway detouring on all the side streets: Forty-fourth, Forty-fifth, Forty-sixth Street, wherever producers or agents had offices.

We learned, too, that actors congregated during the day at the drugstore in the Astor Hotel, and exchanged tips with each other about casting. So John and I made it a habit to go there at least twice a day. We had our lunch there, and soon we made friends who shared tips with us.

The legendary producer Arthur Hopkins had his office on Forty-fourth Street and usually a secretary would be seated in the outer office. One day in the late fall, I entered the office and she wasn't there. Mr. Hopkins himself was seated at her desk, wearing his hat and reading a manuscript. By this time I'd heard a lot about him and his adventurous productions. The sight of him unnerved me so that I almost walked out without saying anything, but I finally got the nerve to ask, "Anything today, Mr. Hopkins?" and not looking up from his reading, he just shook his head no and I said my thank you and went out. I forgot now why John wasn't with me, but he wasn't, and I went looking for him and finding him, in great excitement, yelled, "Guess what happened to me?"

"You have a job?" he yelled back.

"No, but guess who I saw just now in his office?"

"Who?"

"Arthur Hopkins."

"Go on."

"I swear. Go up to his office right now and you'll see him."

"Come on with me," John said.

"No, I can't go back. He'll think I'm crazy. Hurry up, though, he may leave."

I walked with him to the building where Arthur Hopkins had his office and waited in the lobby while he went up to see the great man. He wasn't gone long and as he came out of the elevator I asked, "Did you see him?"

"No," John said. "The office door was locked when I got there."

*   *   *

I met Arthur Hopkins in 1944 when my play *Only the Heart* was done at the Bijou Theater on Forty-fourth Street. The star, June Walker, revered Arthur Hopkins. She invited him to a preview. He liked the play and the production very much and asked to meet me. I knew by then all he had accomplished in the theater as a director and producer and knew, too, that he was supposed to be very taciturn and said very little while directing. A small, round man, he spoke quietly, so quietly I had to strain to hear, but he spoke with great wisdom and one sensed right away that he loved the theater. He had not produced much lately and the theater in those last years had not been kind to him. He was still idolized by an older theater generation, and this is reflected in a letter to him Eugene O'Neill had written about the same time as I met him.

Dear Arthur:

It was grand to hear from you. Many and many a time since my serious illness in '36–'37, I've said to myself I'm going to write Arthur. Not on any particular subject, but in general about the way I felt and I know you must feel about the disappointment of seeing the spirit of the American Theater forget the spirit of the twenties theater for art's sake and drift into all kinds of blind alleys. Theater for socialities sake, partisan politics sake, provincial patriotism's sake and etc. Polly [Pauline Lord] in "Anna Christie" certainly brings back a lot of pleasant memories. I wish I could have heard her in it. I don't think I'm just a man of 55 looking back on the good old days. There was a spirit then that has been lost. There were uncompromising idealists with a real love for what the American Theater might become. If there are such left—with a few exceptions to prove the rule— then I never hear from them. All are from show shop people, and mark that angle as they may with idealistic phrases for my beguiling, that angle is all that they can conceive of as theater. Not that I have any prejudice against show shop people as such, God knows, anymore than I have against pictures, but there should be a theater, too, recognized as separate and an attempt as art, and not judged by the same standards. Or by any propaganda standards.

And again my deep gratitude for all you did for me. That, believe me, I have never forgotten nor can ever forget.

Affectionately, Gene

Just before Thanksgiving, for lack of business, *The Province-town Follies* was forced to close. Joe was in rehearsal with his play and John and I had both saved a little money from our Province-town jobs, but it was fast disappearing. One bitterly cold winter day I was again making the rounds alone, and I was to meet John at four o'clock in the Astor Hotel lobby. I'd had no lunch to save money and had been going from office to office since ten that morning and was exhausted. I looked at my watch and it said three o'clock and if I had an extra nickel I would have gone to a drugstore and had a Coke or some coffee, but I didn't. So I was about to go into the Astor lobby where it was warm and wait for John, when I remembered three agencies farther uptown that I hadn't gone to that day. I decided to see if they had any work. The receptionists at the first two agencies were polite and we dis-cussed the weather and how bitterly cold it was until finally I got around to the eternal question, "Are you casting today?" and they said as always, most politely, "Not today." The second agency was owned by Mrs. Murray Philips and she was always polite and encouraging to actors and I had been disappointed when she hadn't been there. When I got back down to the lobby of her building, I stood looking out the door at Seventh Avenue, debating what to do next when Mrs. Philips came in through the lobby door and spoke to me. She asked, "How are you?"

"Well," I said.

"Have you found any work yet?"

"No."

"Well, don't get discouraged, it all takes time."

"I wasn't," I said. Which was a lie, of course, because though I wouldn't admit it to Mrs. Philips, or anyone else, not Joe or John certainly, and not to my parents, whom I continued to write the most optimistic letters about how much I loved New York and how certain I was to find work soon, I felt bitterly discouraged and frightened, too.

Finally I made myself go back out to Seventh Avenue and looked up the avenue toward Fifty-seventh Street, and debated whether to go to that last office, the Jennie Jacobs Agency. I had never heard of anyone getting a job there, and so I decided to give up for the day and go back to the warmth of the Astor lobby and wait for John. I started back and then I stopped and I said to myself, You've come this far, make one last stop, so I pulled my overcoat collar tight around my neck and started up cold Seventh Avenue toward Fifty-seventh Street.

When I got to the Jacobs office it was empty, but after a moment Henry Weiss, Miss Jacobs's assistant, came in and before I could ask if there were any casting he said, "Nothing today, son, sorry." I was too discouraged to even say thank you and turned to go out, when he suddenly said, "Wait a minute." I stopped and turned around and he looked at me for a moment and then he said, "I'm going to send you over to the Fox Studio near Tenth Avenue. Can you go now?"

I said, "I certainly can." So he wrote out the address and the name of the person I was to ask for, and I took off, practically running all the way.

The Fox Studio was in the Fifties between Nineth and Tenth avenues, and looked more like a Seventh Avenue clothing factory then a film studio, or anyway, what I thought a film studio should look like. I found the person I was to see and he looked me over for about five minutes, all the time my heart racing, expecting him to say no, not right, but he didn't and instead said, "Come with me."

We went inside the studio to a small office covered with posters of Fox films, many that I had never heard of, and he gave me a script and asked me to read for him. I was about to ask him if I could look it over first and he must have anticipated the question for he said, "It's a small part," and pointing to the script said, "It begins here and ends here. You are a fifteenth-century waif and in the scene you are very frightened of the man you are apprenticed to. I'll give you ten minutes." He looked at his watch and went to his desk and began to look over some letters as I read the scene. When the ten minutes was up, he said, "Okay, let's go," and he came back to me and he had a script and I read and there was a pause and my heart again was racing and he said finally, "We're going to shoot tomorrow, are you free?"

"Yessir," I said.

"Well, go home," he said, "and I'll call you by seven o'clock tonight if you have the part." He took my phone number and I practically ran out of his office to the Eighth Avenue subway. All of a sudden everything looked so different. I paid no attention to the cold, and the subway for a change seemed friendly and even cozy.

I got off at the Washington Square stop and ran up the steps of the station and continued running to our apartment on Mac-Dougal Street.

John had the good sense not to wait around when I wasn't at the Astor Hotel at four and was in the apartment when I got there. He had bought a few groceries and was about to fry some hamburgers, when I came in and told him my news. It was six o'clock by then. We had no phone in our apartment and the pay phone for all the tenants was on the fifth floor. I was almost too excited to eat, but I finally managed to get some food down, and I opened the front door of the apartment so I could hear the phone ring, if it did ring, and I was trying to be calm and pretend I didn't care one way or the other, but when five after seven came and there was no ring my heart began to sink. Finally at ten after seven the phone rang and then stopped. Then I began to worry about whether the person answering the phone would know, if it were for me, that I lived in the building. A second more passed, then two, and then three, and I heard someone with an Italian accent shout, "Footie! Footie!" And I began hollering, "I'm here, I'm here," running up the five flights of stairs to the phone. I took the dangling receiver and said, "Yes."

A man's voice said, "Is this Horton Foote?"

"Yes."

"Can you be at the studio at seven in the morning for costume and makeup?"

"Yessir, I certainly can."

"Fine," he said. "I'll see you then."

Joe was home from rehearsal when I got back down to the apartment.

"I got the part," I said out of breath from running up and down five flights of stairs.

"What is the name of the picture?" Joe asked.

"I don't know. No one told me. All I know is I'm to have two or three days of work and I'll be paid a hundred and fifty dollars, and I think I was told Paul Leyssac and Ernest Glendinning are to be in it."

I knew that Ernest Glendinning was a popular Broadway actor and that Paul Leyssac had been a member of the Le Gallienne Company, which of course pleased me, as I still had strong memories of the Ibsen plays and her performance.

I was at the studio promptly at seven. The makeup man confirmed that Ernest Glendinning and Paul Leyssac were to be in the cast. At seven thirty they both arrived and I was introduced to them. Paul Leyssac was tall and distinguished looking with a neatly clipped beard. I had seen him in the Le Gallienne plays in Los Angeles and I remembered particularly his performance in *Hedda Gabler.* I told him how much I enjoyed his acting. He thanked me, but began right away talking to Glendinning. I wanted to say to Mr. Glendinning, a short, slight man, who looked to me more like a bank clerk than an actor, how much I liked his work, but I couldn't because I had never seen him in a play. On the set between shots I had a chance to speak to Leyssac again. I told him how much I admired Miss Le Gallienne and all she stood for in the theater, and how I felt it was a shame her theater had to close.

"It's better closed," he said angrily. "There's no place for it in

New York anymore. It was wasted years as far as I'm concerned. We were all fools thinking it would work. What did we end up with? Nothing. Who cares about us now? It was no life at all. Work. Work. Work. And for what? For nothing." He sighed and then he walked off and avoided me the rest of the time.

My first scene was shot late in the afternoon and I was called back the next day and was through by three o'clock. I still hadn't found out the name of the film or what it was for, but I got my money and I felt like a rich man.

I was sent some stills of my scenes with Mr. Leyssac and Mr. Glendinning but with no mention of the name of the film. Many, many years later, Crystal Brian, working on a biography of me, looked up the film in the film archives at a California university and found it. She said it had been made as an industrial film of some kind to be used for advertising purposes.

A few weeks later my cousin Nan Outlar (whom I sometimes called Nannie in this book) wrote me that Ed Roberts, an old beau of hers from the University of Texas, was working in the New York office of Goldwyn Pictures. She had written him about me and he had asked for me to come to see him at his office. I called him the next day and made an appointment. He was a short, intense man, devoted to Nan, and said he would like to help me in any way he could. Two days later he called to say that the studio was making some screen tests with Milton Berle the comedian and others. They needed an actor to be in the tests with him and asked if I would like the work. It would pay a hundred dollars.

"I certainly would."

Then he laughed and said, "Who knows, they may see the screen test and decide to bring you out to Hollywood instead of Milton Berle, but then Nan tells me you don't want to have anything to do with pictures."

"That's right."

"Well, good for you," he said, "and stick to your guns. The way things are going now, I think in a few years every actor in New York will be heading for Hollywood."

I was at the studio promptly at seven the next morning and was in the makeup room waiting to be made up when Milton Berle and his entourage arrived. There was a lot of joking and general carrying on. His mother was with them and she saw me sitting in the makeup room and told the makeup man to put my makeup on right away. When he had finished and had left the room, she said, "Now, good. You see, son, there is some confusion and we may not do the screen test, but now that you have your makeup on they will have to pay you." In a few minutes Berle called his mother and he and his entourage left and someone from the studio came in and told me it was all off and I could go home, but he said since I had my makeup on I would get paid.

Christmas was approaching and I hadn't been able to find any other work. Joe's play had opened and closed and he was going to his home in Milwaukee for Christmas. I continued to write optimistic letters to my family, and I saw snow for the first time. It started snowing early in the morning and lasted all day. John didn't want to look for work in the snow, but I said I was going to, which made him feel guilty about not going, I suppose, for just as I got to the subway I heard him call, "Wait for me!"

The snow was lovely, a slow, gentle snow, and when I told John how much warmer it was even with the snow, he explained that snow always does that.

I wrote my parents a long letter that night describing the snow, which they had only seen once in our Texas town before I was born, and a sight my father never got tired of telling about.

Few offices were open because of the snowstorm, so John and I went home early and I found two packages waiting for me. One from my cousin Nan Outlar containing cans of food that she knew I liked. The other package was from my Aunt Lily Coffee, my father's sister, with a letter explaining that she was very discouraged because no one in Houston was able to help get her musical compositions published and she was sending twelve of them to me in the hope that I would meet someone in New York that might be interested.

John had a letter, too, from his brother sending money for bus fare to Lock Haven for Christmas. He asked me if I would like to spend Christmas with him. He explained that he couldn't have me stay with his family as they had no extra room, but Bucknell was only a few miles away in Lewisburg and he was sure a professor he knew would have room for me and would welcome me.

We arrived in Lock Haven on Christmas Eve. It was a gray, dreary day, and bitterly cold. John's brother was there at the bus station to meet us, a shy, thin man wearing glasses and beginning to lose his hair.

He and John shook hands and we were introduced and shook hands. He said, "John, you can use the car if you'll first drop me off at my office." John thanked him. John's brother then asked if he could carry my suitcase and I thanked him, but said I could manage. We walked in silence to his car, a Ford that had seen better days. As we were getting in, he apologized for the untidiness of the car and asked, "Can you drive?"

"No."

"That's strange, I thought everybody in Texas drove cars."

"That is just about so, but I can't."

The apartment John's family lived in was on the first floor of a wood building badly needing paint. John's mother and sister-in-law and her son, three, were waiting for us in the living room. The room was small and crowded with furniture. When John and I entered the room he didn't kiss his mother or even shake her hand. He just said, "Mama, this is my friend Horton."

She nodded without speaking, nor did she extend her hand in greeting. John's mother had the saddest face I think I've ever seen.

When he introduced me to his sister-in-law and his nephew, the sister-in-law said, "Hi," and the little boy buried his head in his mother's lap and said nothing. There was an awkward pause then and no one said anything at all.

Finally John said, "I'm going to take Horton over to Professor Giese's now. I'm having dinner with them and I may come in late, so don't wait up for me."

They didn't comment about that and I said finally, "It was nice meeting you."

The mother said nothing, but gave me a warm smile, and the sister-in-law said, "Likewise," and we left.

Professor Giese's apartment in the town of Lewisburg was spacious and pleasant. He was German, and had only been in America for ten years, but by now had little accent. He had been in the German army, conscripted when he was seventeen and wounded, his left arm shriveled and useless.

John asked Professor Giese if he would look at my aunt's music, which I had brought with me. That night after John had gone home he took her music into his study.

The next morning over breakfast he said, "Well, she is not without talent, your aunt, but unfortunately it has been ruined by sentimentality." He asked me about her and about my family and Texas and then he told me about Germany and his war experiences.

The next day it snowed and I began to feel anxious about being away from New York, so I called John and said I thought I'd go on back early after I had Christmas dinner. He didn't try to get me to stay, nor did Professor Giese.

John came for me at eleven Christmas morning and he said his mother had been taken sick and had to go to the hospital, so his family wasn't having Christmas dinner and we'd have to eat at a restaurant. He said his brother had given him some money to pay for our dinner. John drove me back to his house after the meal and I got my suitcase and took the next bus for New York.

I got into New York City at around eleven at night. I woke up early the next morning and dressed to make the rounds, but when I looked out the window and I saw a fierce snowstorm in progress, I decided to stay in the apartment. A package came in the afternoon from my mother and father. They sent me a shirt, a pair of socks, a tie, a fruit cake, and a box of Christmas cookies.

* * *

Our apartment was over a small nightclub called the Welcome Inn. It had a three-piece orchestra, piano, drums, and saxophone that started playing at around eight every night and continued until twelve. "I'm in the Mood for Love" must have been a great favorite with their customers because they seemed to play it over and over. Usually I paid no attention to the orchestra, but this night I became very aware of it, and I was happy when twelve came and the music ended.

The snow had stopped by the next day, so I took the subway to Forty-second Street and dutifully began the rounds. The first office I went into was Jane Broder's. She was considered by actors I knew to be the best of the theater agents. I had never been to her office before, but this morning I felt adventurous and I decided to make a visit.

Inside Miss Broder's office was a lady, rather stout, at a desk reading a manuscript. I thought it must be her secretary, and I went up to her.

"Excuse me," I said.

"Yes?" the lady said.

"I'm here to see Miss Jane Broder."

"I'm Jane Broder," she said.

"Oh." I was so thrown by that I couldn't think what to say next.

"Are you an actor?" Miss Broder asked.

"Yes, ma'am."

"I don't know your work, do I?"

"I don't think so."

"What have you done?" she asked, almost sternly it seemed to me.

"I'm a graduate of the Pasadena Playhouse," I said.

I was about to tell her of my experience in a film when she asked me, "Have you been in a play in New York?"

"No."

Again I was about to tell her of my film experience, but before I could get a word out she said, "Well, when you're in a play, drop me a card and I'll try to come and see you."

"Yes, ma'am. Thank you."

I started away and she called, "Young man."

I stopped, and I thought maybe this will be like Henry Weiss, and I'll be sent out for a job.

"Yes, ma'am."

"You've just come to New York?"

"No, ma'am. I've been here three months," and I added hurriedly, "I got a job doing props at the Provincetown Playhouse, then a small part in a movie and—"

"Young man," she interrupted me. "Do you realize this is Christmas week and you're wasting your time tramping around in the snow and the cold during Christmas week? There is absolutely nothing going on. Take it from me. You are wasting subway fare looking for theater work this week of all weeks."

She went back to her reading then and I went out the door as quietly as I could.

I spent New Year's Eve alone. The orchestra in the club below played that night until four in the morning and I was kept awake listening to "I'm in the Mood for Love," "Dream a Little Dream of Me," "I'll Get By," and other popular songs played over and over and over. When they played "Red Sails in the Sunset," a song which had been featured in *The Provincetown Follies,* I went outside the apartment and crossed the street to the Provincetown

Playhouse, all boarded up and looking very desolate and forlorn. I looked back across the street at the Welcome Inn with its fair-size crowd. Everyone seemed in a festive mood and I was tempted to go in and buy a beer to celebrate the new year, but I knew I had better not spend the money. I went back into my apartment and wrote to my family, thanking them for my presents and telling them, lying of course, what a wonderful Christmas I'd had in Lock Haven with John and with what confidence I felt now that my career would take off for sure in this new year.

When I finished I made myself a cup of coffee and cut myself a piece of fruit cake and sat eating it, drinking my coffee and listening to the music of the three-piece band in the Welcome Inn.

CHAPTER 8

Andrius Jilinsky   *Madame Soloviova*

In January 1936, Pauline Lord opened in Edith Wharton's *Ethan Frome* at the National Theater. It received wonderful notices from the daily papers. Stark Young in *The New Republic* began his review this way:

> No matter what the outcome may be, an event in the theater, may differ almost generically from the majority of events, for the mere reason of some presence in it, be that actor, dramatist or what not. When Miss Lord appears in a realistic piece, no matter how inferior the play may be, it should be taken as a theatrical event of the first rank.

Ruth Gordon and Raymond Massey were in the play, too, and I decided it was something I wanted to see. I had gone to the theater as often as I could since I'd been in New York, buying a seat in the second balcony for fifty-five cents. I had already learned the trick of looking down from the second balcony at the orchestra below, just before the house lights dimmed, to see if there were any unsold seats, and if there were, going down after the first intermission to take one of them. I'd seen, starting from the balcony, *Winterset* with Burgess Meredith and Margo, *The Old Maid* with Judith Anderson and Helen Menken, Lillian Hellman's *The Children's Hour*, *Kind Lady* with Grace George, Sidney Kingsley's *Dead End* and *Remember the Day,* all popular plays of the day with popular actresses and actors, and from the orchestra, taken by a friend, Nazimova's powerful performance as Mrs. Alving in Ibsen's *Ghosts.* For some reason, though, I felt even if I had to pay, I wanted to see *Ethan Frome* from the very beginning in the orchestra. I went to a matinee and I thought long and hard before finally paying three dollars and sixty cents for an orchestra ticket. I had not read the Edith Wharton novel the play was based on, but I knew it was a favorite of many of my friends. I was shown to my seat by an usher and began to read my program when the house lights dimmed and there was the usual hush in the theater before a play started.

Ethan Frome is set in the early twentieth century in rural New England. Ethan and Zenobia Frome have been married a number of years. She is an invalid constantly making Ethan or anyone around aware of that fact. Their life is a hard one. What little they have comes from his farming land that is poor and unyielding. The winters are long and severe. Zenobia, from a neighboring town, had been hired by Ethan to nurse his mentally unstable mother. The day of the mother's funeral, Ethan, fearing being left alone, asks Zenobia to stay and marry him. She agrees. They have been married seven years when Zenobia asks to bring in Mattie Silver, a distant cousin who is penniless, to live with them and take over the cooking and the housework. Ethan says he can't afford feeding another person, but Zenobia finally gets her way and Mattie is sent for. Mattie, young, cheerful, and outgoing, soon wins Ethan's friendship and love. Zenobia, seeing their growing attraction, arranges for a hired girl to replace Mattie, insisting that Mattie leave the farm. Ethan refuses at first to allow this, but finally is forced to give in. He convinces Mattie that death is preferable to their being separated and arranges a sledding accident that will kill them both. Instead, because of Ethan's miscalculation, they are not killed, but Mattie is paralyzed and confined to a wheelchair. The three are forced to live together, Zenobia now nursing the helpless Mattie as she did Ethan's mother.

Ruth Gordon was interesting as Mattie Silver and Raymond Massey effective as Ethan, but it was Miss Lord, who, from her first entrance, drab in her costume, whining her complaints quietly and subtly, moment by unforced moment, created a life onstage I have never forgotten. She spared us none of the complaining and hypochondria of her character, but through the genius of her acting she made us aware, too, of all the complexities of this tragic and unhappy woman.

Stark Young in his review of her performance wrote:

Miss Lord clears the whole thing up and tops everything, the story, the play, the scene, the acting. There are things here that Mrs. Wharton for all her ability and confidence in approach, could not ever have imagined. By what process is it in Miss Lord's portrayal that her opening of a door and standing there—or any of that continued perfection of her playing—can begin our entrance into a realm that we cannot explain, nor predict technically, nobody can say. Her performance has a miraculous humility, a subtle variety and a gradation and shy power that are undescribable. Of this art of Pauline Lord's, you know that its still small voice haunts your ears and its weaknesses overpowers you, as you go back to it in your thoughts, thoughts tender and somewhat owned by that of which you have heard only the echo.

Echoes of her performance indeed still come to me after all these years. A performance I consider the most moving I have ever seen.

Late January there was a thaw and the winter suddenly receded and I felt finally it might be over. Joe and John, used to the cold climates of Wisconsin and Pennsylvania, kept telling me it wasn't and not to get my hopes up.

Since his return from Lock Haven, John was now looking less and less for acting jobs, and began reading the want ads for temporary work. The agencies for these jobs were on Sixth Avenue and I knew in time, a very short time now, if I didn't find theater work I would have to join him on his Sixth Avenue job search.

On a still, warm January day I was walking down Broadway and I thought I saw Rosamond Pinchot. We were walking toward each other but we were still a distance apart, when she turned away and went into a drugstore.

I got to the drugstore as quickly as I could, went in, and

looked around and finally saw her over at a far counter. I had a moment of wondering if she would remember me since it had been nearly a year since I'd seen her in Pasadena.

"Rosamond," I said almost hesitantly, as I walked toward her. She turned around at the sound of her name and saw me, smiled, and said, "Horton." I went over to her then as quickly as I could.

"What are you up to?" I asked.

"I'm studying with the Russians," she said. "I was with Ouspenskaya, but she's closed her studio and gone to Hollywood. Tamara Daykarhanova, though, has opened a studio and that's where I'm working. I need a scene partner and if you'd be interested I'd pay your tuition and we could work on scenes together. I'm anxious to work on *Candida.* Would you be interested in working with me?"

"Yes, I certainly would."

"All right. I'll arrange with Daykarhanova. Classes are from two to four, Tuesdays and Fridays. Can you start tomorrow?"

"Yes. What is the address?"

"Fifty-five West Fifty-sixth Street. Between Fifth and Sixth avenues."

I arrived promptly at one forty-five and Rosamond greeted me.

"I'm glad you're here," she said. "Come on, I want you to meet Frances Deitz."

I followed her into a small office and she knocked on the door at the far end and a woman's voice called out, "Come in." Rosamond opened the door and I could see a desk and two chairs, and seated at the desk was a small, petite woman in her early thirties with intense black or brown eyes and jet-black hair pulled tightly and gathered in a knot at the back of her head. She was smoking a cigarette and when she saw Rosamond, said, "Yes, Rosamond?"

"I have my friend with me, Frances, who I want to enroll," Rosamond said, as we stood in the doorway.

"Where is he?" Frances asked.

"Right here," Rosamond said, pointing to me.

"Oh," Frances said, looking me over in a manner that I felt was very disapproving. "Has he met Madame?"

"No. But I spoke to her about him this morning and she said to tell you it has her approval. He's going to be my scene partner this month at least."

"Oh. Very well." There was another pause while she again looked me over. "Come on in. What's your name?"

"Horton Foote," I said, walking into the room.

"Do you need me, too?" Rosamond asked.

"No," Frances said.

"I'll meet you in the studio," Rosamond said.

She left and Miss Deitz looked at some papers on her desk and then looked up at me and said, "Close the door, please," and I did. She pointed to a chair and said, "Sit down, please." Again I did as I was told and waited while she continued to look me over. Finally after putting out one cigarette in an ashtray and lighting another she asked, "How long have you known Rosamond?"

"Well, let's see," I said. "Not too long, really. I met her in Pasadena."

"Were you at the playhouse?" she asked.

"Yes," I said.

"At the school there?" she asked with a look of despair.

"Yes," I said.

She sighed and shook her head.

"Does Madame know this?"

"I don't know," I said.

A woman, maybe fifty-five, with dark hair, cut short, wearing a silk blouse and a tailored skirt, her eyes brown as Miss Deitz's, a pointed chin, her face unwrinkled, came into the office, her head held slightly to one side.

"Madame Daykarhanova," Miss Deitz said, lighting another cigarette. "This is the friend of Rosamond's that she spoke to you about."

"Yes," Madame said, looking me up and down.

"Did she tell you where they met?" Miss Deitz continued.

"No," Madame said.

"In Pasadena. At the playhouse." Miss Deitz spoke with an ominous tone in her voice.

"Pasadena," Madame repeated. It was quite clear now when she said the word *Pasadena* she had quite an accent. "Did you play parts there?"

Before I could answer, Miss Deitz said, "He went to school there."

"Oh," Madame said. "You studied there?"

"Yes, ma'am."

"How old are you?" Madame asked, not unkindly.

"Nineteen," I said.

"Well, and you want to study with me?"

"Yes," I said, although I really wanted to say I don't really know, I thought I was just here to do scenes with Rosamond.

"Good," she said. "You are to work with Rosamond on scenes?"

"I believe so," I said.

"Good," Madame continued. "You know we don't teach here

like they do at Pasadena Playhouse. We are very strict here. Very, very strict. Isn't that right, Miss Deitz?"

"Yes, Madame," Miss Deitz agreed.

"And you are willing to work hard?" Madame Daykarhanova said, looking directly into my eyes, as if she could tell by so doing if my answer was truthful or not.

"Yes, ma'am," I said.

"You understand, you will have to forget everything you learned at Pasadena school," she said again, not unkindly, but firmly. "And you're willing to do this?"

"Yes," I said, not really knowing what she was talking about. "I am."

"Good," she said. "It's not always easy, you know, getting rid of old ways." She paused then, looked at me closely once more, and then sighed and said to Miss Deitz, "Do you need him anymore?"

"No," Miss Deitz said. "Class is in ten minutes."

There were several students there, all so involved in their conversations that they weren't aware of me at all. Rosamond saw me then and came over to me.

"You met Madame?" she asked.

"Yes," I said.

She started down the hall as a woman with reddish hair, obviously dyed, wearing a smock, and with the largest most beautiful light brown eyes I'd ever seen, came out of what I was to know in time as the makeup room.

"Hello, Rosamond," she said, her accent as pronounced as Madame Daykarhanova's.

"Hello, Madame," Rosamond said. "Madame, this is Horton Foote. He's here to work on scenes with me."

"Good," she said, smiling. "Good. Very good."

"Madame Balieff teaches makeup."

Madame Balieff laughed at that as if Rosamond had told a joke.

"Will you study makeup?" Madame Balieff asked.

"I don't think so," I said.

"He's here to do scenes with me," Rosamond said.

"Oh." Madame Balieff sighed, and then said, "Nice to have met you."

"Nice to have met you," I said.

Rosamond continued walking down the hall and I followed.

"Madame Balieff was married to the famous Russian director Komisarjevsky," Rosamond said. "They were divorced and then she married Nikita Balieff, who produced the *Chauve Souris*. Madame Daykarhanova was one of the stars of the *Chauve Souris*." I wanted to ask, What in the world is the *Chauve Souris*, but I didn't.

The studio was a very long, narrow room and near the entrance were two large upholstered chairs and around them were twelve or more straight chairs.

"That's where Madames Daykarhanova and Soloviova sit," Rosamond said, pointing to the two upholstered chairs. "We sit in these," she added, pointing to the straight chairs. "Let's sit here," she said. "Near the madames; because of their accents it's a little hard understanding them sometimes."

"Who is Madame Soloviova?" I asked.

"Oh. Well, she's married to Mr. Jilinsky, who teaches acting technique in the mornings. They're both from the Art Theater."

Again I wanted to ask what's the Art Theater, but I didn't.

"They both came here with the Michael Chekhov Company, and when it disbanded stayed on in New York to teach."

I found out later that the Art Theater Rosamond spoke of that day was the Moscow Art Theater, and that the Michael Chekhov Soloviova and Jilinsky came to America with was the nephew of Anton Chekhov. Michael Chekhov was considered by all my Russian teachers and friends a very great actor, director, and teacher.

Students began to drift in now, usually in pairs, talking as they entered, greeting each other and waving to Rosamond. Promptly at two o'clock, Madame Daykarhanova and Madame Soloviova entered. Madame Soloviova first, also wearing a silk blouse and a tailored skirt. She had a round, lovely face and blue eyes and was smiling as she entered. Madame Daykarhanova followed, smiling, too, now, and they seated themselves in their chairs and began to speak to each other in Russian, laughing quite loudly at one point at something Madame Soloviova said.

When they finished their conversation, Madame Daykarhanova lit a cigarette and with a piercing look, that in time would become very familiar to me, looked slowly over the students, finally saying, "Who has scene for today?" Five of the students raised their hands, she looked at them for a moment, and then turned to Madame Soloviova and again speaking in Russian, they conferred for a minute or so. Then Madame Daykarhanova turned back to the students, and told the order in which the scenes would be seen. The two girls she called on first got up and walked to the far end of the room, and began to move some chairs and tables to make a setting for their scene.

"Begin when you're ready," Madame Daykarhanova said.

The girls finished arranging the furniture and then both turned away from each other and were very still and silent. I thought for a moment they were praying, but then suddenly they turned toward each other and took places in the space they had created and began their scene.

I don't remember what that scene was or the names of any of the others given that day, but I do remember hearing for the first time strange phrases used by the two madames when criticizing—*actions, beats, wants, concentration, sense memory, preparations, through line, spine, subtext, really listening, really seeing, colors, real, truthful, old-fashioned acting, acting clichés*—phrases I was to hear a great deal of in the days and weeks ahead.

Before giving criticism of a scene, Madame Soloviova and Madame Daykarhanova would converse in Russian. Then Daykarhanova would speak first in English, followed by Soloviova who spoke English with a much heavier accent, but in contrast to Daykarhanova's stern look as she spoke to the students, Soloviova had a perpetual smile as she talked and her blue eyes at times literally twinkled. She could be as severe in her opinions as Daykarhanova, but she never seemed angry while giving them as sometimes Daykarhanova did.

Everyone that did scenes that day seemed to understand the acting terms, so foreign to me at the time, used by the teachers. At the end of the class, Daykarhanova asked what scenes would be ready for the next session and hands were raised and scenes promised, then Daykarhanova turned to Rosamond and asked when our scene from *Candida* would be ready, and Rosamond said she hoped by the end of the week.

Rosamond and I made a date to meet the next afternoon at her house on the Upper East Side. I was a little early and walked around the block a number of times before going up a small flight of steps to a glass door with a screen of black metal mesh covering it. I found a bell, rang it. After a few minutes I heard a buzzer and realized I was now to open the door, but I realized it too late. I had to ring the bell again and this time kept my hand on the handle of the door. Rosamond was entering the front hall as I opened the door. She greeted me warmly and said, pointing to a parlor, "Let's work in here." I followed her into a very elegant room, handsomely furnished. "Usually I work upstairs in the study," she said, "but we're having painting done there today and since we'll only be reading, I thought we could manage in here. Anyway, it may be some time before we can actually do the scene in class as I've just found out I have to go out to Hollywood to see about a movie, which I probably won't get. I'll be back in a week or so. Let's read the scene, just simply, just for sense, and see how it goes."

I arrived at the studio twenty minutes before two on Friday and when I got off the elevator Madame Daykarhanova was walking down the hall. She saw me and she called out, "Horton."

I was startled that she knew my name and I waited as she came up to me.

"Horton," she said. "Rosamond called an hour ago and has to

leave right away for Hollywood. She's very distressed she's deserting you and promises to be back as soon as she can. In the meantime, since she has paid tuition for you, if you want to stay I will be happy for you to."

"Well, thank you," I said. "I'd like to."

And so began my years with the Russians. Besides Madame Daykarhanova and Madame Soloviova and Madame Balieff, there was Madame Boleslavsky, the ex-wife of Richard Boleslavsky. He and Madame Ouspenskaya were the first Russians from the Moscow Art Theater to come to New York to teach. Although I never knew Madame Ouspenskaya or Richard Boleslavsky, I felt I had because they were both quoted so much and so often by Daykarhanova and Soloviova, and by a number of students who had studied at their studio, or had been in plays directed by Boleslavsky. Boleslavsky's book, *Acting: The First Six Lessons,* had become a kind of primer for young actors.

John Forsht had not been able to find even a temporary job and had gone back to Lock Haven to work and save some money. Joe and I felt the MacDougal apartment was too expensive for just the two of us so we decided each should get his own room in a rooming house. I found a small one I could afford on West Seventieth Street, with a hot plate for cooking.

Rosamond Pinchot didn't come back from Hollywood that year, and I didn't see her again until we both had jobs the following year in Max Reinhardt's *The Eternal Road.* When I heard Rosamond wouldn't be back, I thought I would have to leave the school, but Miss Deitz called me into the office and said, "If you want to stay on here at school, Madame will give you a scholarship, and to pay for it you can help me in the office, and run the elevator when the regular man is off-duty. Madame always has a recital at the end of the semester and this is a chance to have your work seen by agents and producers, and it might lead to a job. Madame feels, too, that Mr. Jilinsky's classes in techniques will be helpful to you, and she would like you to take them."

"What does that mean, technique?" I asked.

"Acting technique," she said. I must have still looked puzzled because she added, "Exercises, sensory work, concentration, all the tools an actor needs. His classes are in the mornings. Five days a week. Your friend Joe Anthony is going into his class. He signed up this morning, and some other people from Pasadena you know are joining, Mary Virginia Palmer and Patricia Coates. Shall I sign you up?" Miss Deitz asked impatiently.

"Oh, yes."

I pretended to be very grateful and excited, but in truth I had no idea of what I was getting into.

It is difficult now to realize how unique, revolutionary even, Andrius Jilinsky's approach to the training of the actor was when I began studying with him in 1935. Only Jilinsky, working with his wife, Madame Soloviova, and Madame Daykarhanova, was teaching on any regular basis what had been taught by Stanislavsky at the Moscow Art Theater. Jilinsky was an inspired teacher. A tall, vigorous, handsome man with a booming voice, I can hear him even now challenging, inspiring his students to a larger sense of theater and theater practice than their own undernourished, conventional American training had allowed.

He loved teaching and he was patient and kind even to the least talented of his students. And he was generous with his knowledge to all of our young (and not so young) clamoring egos.

A refugee from Stalinist Russia, loving that country, its language, its cultural heritage, but despising the political tyranny he thought so destructive and coming to America with little knowledge of our language, our customs, or our theater, he seemed to have been in an extremely precarious position. And yet he never brought bitterness or self-pity to his classes or to his students. If he talked of Russia, it was never of the politics that had so cruelly disrupted his life, but of the Moscow Art Theater, Stanislavsky, Chekhov, Gorki, and Tolstoy.

What he taught I now realize was a combination of what he had learned from Stanislavsky and from his work with Michael Chekhov.

In a letter to the playwright Lynn Riggs, he wrote early in the 1930s:

Dear Lynn Riggs:
In the accepted triangle of the theater—playwright, director and actor—it seems to me that the ideal of collaboration forms an equilateral triangle. If there is no playwrighting for and from the theater, there is no theater. If there is no actor especially "created" and trained to fulfill the tasks of the theater, there is no theater. And if there is no director who understands how to produce the plays of these playwrights with these actors, there is no theater.

I translate from the Russian of Pushkin one of his sayings

about the kind of acting that must be in the theater. "Verity of passion, verisimilitude of the feelings in the given circumstances." It is not simplicity for the sake of simplicity. If you understand the system that way you only vulgarize it. It is something else, something very different and responsible. If you want to create truth on the stage, you must be acquainted with your own truth, and the truth of your life. It is something that belongs not only to the tradition of acting, but to the moral content of the theater. Here lies the secret of the living theater, which gives an inexhaustible source of creative power and makes the theater a constructive force in life.

In Daykarhanova and Soloviova's classes we were preparing scenes for the coming recital. I was to do *Ah, Wilderness* with Betty Goddard, who lived on Park Avenue and whose mother was a friend of Arthur Hopkins and sometimes played bridge with Pauline Lord. I also had become close friends with Perry Wilson, a young actress of great vitality and charm.

She and I talked about doing a scene together and I suggested *The No 'Count Boy.* She read it, liked it, and we rehearsed it and brought it into class. Both Soloviova and Daykarhanova were quite taken with it and said we would also do that in the recital, without blackface. A number of agents and producers attended the recital, among them Arthur Hopkins. Someone from the Warner Brothers New York office was there, too, and spoke to me afterward and said that Warner Brothers would be producing plays next season in New York and that he felt there would be surely a part for me in one of them. Perry Wilson also got work from our scene. She was signed for the summer for the Ann Arbor Festival of plays in Michigan. Later she toured with Pauline Lord in summer theaters in a revival of *The Late Christopher Bean,* and went on from there to job after job in the commercial theater.

I went back to Martha's Vineyard for the summer to work with Miss Townsend, but I was only there a month when I had a call from Warner Brothers to come to New York to start rehearsals for *Swing Your Lady,* one of the plays they were producing.

When I got back to New York I went immediately to the Warner Brothers office and found out the play had been in rehearsal for several weeks. They had not brought in the actors in smaller parts until now to save money.

I reported for rehearsal at the theater the next morning at nine and met Ben Edwards, one of the assistant stage managers. We got to talking and I told him that I was from Texas and he asked, "Where in Texas?"

"Oh, a town you probably never heard of."

"Try me, I know Texas. I have an aunt living there."

"Wharton."

"I've visited there twice," he said. "Do you know my aunt, Mrs. Dave Dickson?"

"Yes, I do. Her husband is my father's best friend."

The stage manager came up then and Ben said, "This is Horton Foote," and we shook hands and he said to Ben, "Give him his sides and go through the part with him, show him where he enters, and describe the kind of energy he has to bring onstage."

The stage manager left and Ben took me onstage and said, "You don't move around at all. You just come in from downstage right and go directly to here and you give your speech and then leave." The stage manager then asked him to work with another actor and he left me alone. After a moment he came back and said, "I forgot to tell you, sit out front this morning. We'll have a run-through of the play and another stage manager will read your part and the other small parts that haven't been rehearsed, and then this afternoon we'll put you into the play for the afternoon run-through."

"Don't I get to rehearse it, before I do the run-through?" I asked.

"No. This is a cheap outfit. None of the actors with small parts get a rehearsal."

"Should I memorize my part?"

"No. Just read it today," he said.

I went out into the auditorium, and I looked around and saw ten or more actors there, and I thought they all seemed so calm, when one of the actors, an older man maybe in his forties, came up to me.

"How are you?" he asked.

"Okay."

"I'm pissed off myself," he said. "I've never heard of such a cheap operation. Did you sign a contract?"

"No."

"Neither have I. And you won't sign one either until you go through the five days."

"What five days?" I asked.

"You don't know about the five days?"

"No."

"Aren't you an Equity member?" he asked.

"No," I said.

"Do they know you're not an Equity member?" he asked.

"Yes. They said I could join after I signed my contract."

"*If* you get a contract," he said dolefully.

"What do you mean?" I asked, becoming alarmed.

"You have to rehearse five days free," he said. "If they don't like you, they can fire you at the end of the five days without paying you a cent."

"Oh."

"You didn't know that?"

"No."

"Well, don't worry about it," he said. "You'll do fine and they'll give you a contract."

But I didn't do fine. I had the worst stage fright I've ever known when I was called onstage to take my place for the run-through. I had hoped to memorize my part to impress them, but I couldn't remember a word when my cue came, and when I went onstage my hand was shaking so I could hardly hold my sides. I had no energy and I'm sure I couldn't be heard beyond the first row. When I left the stage I felt sick, and wasn't surprised when another assistant stage manager, not Ben Edwards, came to tell me he was sorry but the management was going to replace me and would I mind leaving now.

Swing Your Lady opened ten days later, got terrible reviews, and closed in two days. I didn't see Ben Edwards again until 1954 when he was hired to do the set for my play *The Traveling Lady* with Kim Stanley at the Playhouse Theater. We talked about Wharton and his aunt and uncle then, too, but we didn't either of us mention *Swing Your Lady*.

* * *

When I went back to Daykarhanova's in the fall, Benjamin Zemach, whose production of *Salome* I had seen and admired in Pasadena, was attending our classes as an observer.

One day after Jilinsky's class, Zemach came up to me and said that he was doing the choreography for a play by Franz Werfel, called *The Eternal Road*, a story of the Jews' wanderings during the centuries to be directed by Max Reinhardt. It was also a history of the Jewish race, he said, and many of the stories from the Old Testament would be dramatized. He said he wanted good actors to be used along with his dancers, and though none of the actors would have lines, they would be essential to establishing the reality of the various scenes. The pay was twenty-five dollars a week and he hoped I would agree to join the company.

"I thank you," I said. "I will be happy to."

Rehearsals began in mid-October and the play, a spectacle, was to open New Year's Day 1937.

Zemach was an intense, passionate man, and when he would speak to the actors and dancers of what he wanted to accomplish in a given scene, his voice would rise almost to an angry shout as he searched for the English words to explain his ideas. I was in eight scenes in all. The longest concerned the worship of the golden calf by the Israelites in defiance of God's edict against idolatry. The scene ended in an orgy, with the worshipers writhing in erotic ecstasy. All of us in the ensemble (we were never called extras) were in various scenes, sometimes Egyptians, sometimes Hebrews.

Three weeks before opening we left our rehearsal hall to join the full company at the Manhattan Theater on Thirty-fourth Street.

I had read about Reinhardt's production and had heard so much about him from Rosamond Pinchot that I was eagerly looking forward to watching him work. We had been told by Zemach that Reinhardt, many of the actors, and Kurt Weill, the composer, were now refugees from Hitler's Germany.

The day we joined the company there was a great deal of confusion, and we were asked to sit at the back of the theater until we were needed. The Manhattan Theater was a huge barn of a theater and our seats were so far back that I could tell very little of what was going on. The huge, impressive set by Norman Bel Geddes with many ramps was already in place. I recognized Reinhardt from his photographs. Everyone seemed to be speaking German.

When it was time for the dancers and the extras to use the stage, Zemach took over the rehearsal.

As I was walking down to the stage I passed Rosamond Pinchot, who was to play Bathsheba in the production. She came over to me.

"I'm glad you're in the company," she said. "I think you'll learn a great deal from watching Reinhardt at work. We all will."

"I think so. I'm looking forward to it," I said.

"One day when things are quieter I'll take you to meet Reinhardt."

"Thank you," I said. "I would appreciate that."

"And as soon as rehearsals are over and we're playing we'll have dinner together one night."

"I'd like that," I said.

"You're still studying at Daykarhanova's, I understand."

"Yes. Thanks to you."

"No thanks to me."

Rehearsals never got less hectic, and Rosamond I'm sure forgot her promise to introduce me to Reinhardt.

When I got on the stage, I looked out into the auditorium to see if Reinhardt was still there, but I couldn't see him, until one of the other actors in the ensemble pointed to him in a corner of the auditorium talking to someone. I asked my friend if he knew who he was talking to and he said it was Kurt Weill the composer. Every rehearsal I continued to watch for Reinhardt and tried to listen to what he was saying to the actors, or the others working on the production, but he usually spoke in German to the actors from Germany and his English was so hard to understand that I got nothing from it. The show was technically complex and difficult to bring together, but gradually it began to take shape. It was visually very beautiful, and Kurt Weill's score was haunting.

The Eternal Road opened as scheduled on New Year's Day 1937. The reviews were mixed but we were assured by Zemach that the production would last at least until spring.

After a performance one night I met Rosamond as I was leaving. We had spoken briefly several times during rehearsals and had planned to work again on scenes together at Daykarhanova's. When we met this night she said, "I apologize for not being in touch with you, but I've been extremely busy. Jed Harris is waiting for me at the stage door. You know him?" and I said, "I know about him, of course, but we've never met."

Jed Harris was considered one of the most talented director-producers of that time. Among his productions were *The Green Bay Tree, Uncle Vanya,* and later *Our Town.* He was waiting just inside the stage door. He was much younger than I had imagined, and I thought very handsome. If he were an actor, I said to myself, he would be the leading man of the company.

Rosamond seemed very happy when she saw him and I thought to myself, What a great beauty she is, why isn't she getting any important parts in the New York theater? Maybe he will help her.

"Jed," she said. "This is Horton Foote. A friend of mine and a very talented actor. I hope you'll have a part for him one day."

He bowed his head ever so slightly and smiled, but he made no comment. Then he turned to Rosamond and said, "Are you ready?"

"Nice to have met you, sir," I called out to him as they walked out. He turned then and smiled again.

"Thank you," he said.

I never saw or heard from Rosamond again. Late January of the following year I was in the office at Daykarhanova's doing some chores for Miss Deitz when she came in with *The New York Times.* She seemed very upset.

"Horton," she said. "I have something very sad to tell you. Rosamond Pinchot is dead."

"She's what?"

"She's dead. Madame is very distressed. It is all so sad." She handed me the *Times.* "Look on the front page," she said.

I took the paper from her and there on the front page was a headline announcing her death, and in smaller print saying she had taken her life. She was thirty-three years old. She had been helping arrange the sound effects for *Our Town,* directed by Jed Harris, and trying out on the road.

Madame Daykarhanova came in then.

"It is all so sad," she said. "All that beauty. So young. All that beauty. And talent. Much more than she ever realized. Much more."

Besides performing at nights in *The Eternal Road,* I was going to my technique classes with Jilinsky every day and to my scene classes with Daykarhanova and Soloviova twice a week in the afternoons.

Madame Daykarhanova had asked Betty Goddard and me to work on a scene from Lynn Riggs's *Cherokee Nights.* My character, half Cherokee, was being held in jail on suspicion of murder. The sheriff had no direct proof of my committing the crime so they sent a prostitute, played by Betty, into the cell to try to get me to confess. We rehearsed the scene and brought it to class. The scene went well and after the madames finished criticizing, they began to whisper in Russian. When they had finished their whispering they both turned and stared at me for several minutes, when finally Madame Daykarhanova spoke.

"Horton," she said very solemnly. "Madame Soloviova and I have been talking and we think you should now work on Chekhov's *The Sea Gull* with Frances Anderson."

In all the time I had been studying I'd heard many requests from students to let them work on a scene from Chekhov, but permission was never given.

"What scene do you want us to work on?" I asked.

Daykarhanova said very solemnly, "The scene between Nina and Trepliov. Their last scene together."

I looked over at Frances Anderson, small of stature, with very large eyes and a most expressive face. She seemed as surprised as I had been at their request.

"Madame," Frances finally spoke.

"Which one?" Daykarhanova asked.

"Either one," Frances giggled.

Daykarhanova looked at Soloviova and they spoke to each other in Russian; finally Daykarhanova turned away from Soloviova and laughed.

"Vera says don't be afraid. You have capacity to do the scene and I agree."

Frances sighed and smiled a grateful smile.

What about me? I thought. I immediately assumed the scene was being done for Frances.

"Both of you have," she added, as if reading my thoughts.

Frances Anderson was in her late twenties. I had watched her work and realized early on that she was talented, with great emotional range. She was also an accomplished musician. She was making a living now arranging music and playing piano for a Latin band, Mexican or Cuban, I've forgotten which.

The scene we were to work on, the last scene in the play, makes great emotional demands on the actress playing Nina, and on the actor playing Trepliov. After a number of years Nina, who Trepliov is still in love with, returns unexpectedly to his home. The scene for Nina is almost wholly an anguished account of her tragic life since she saw him last. He makes futile attempts to console her, and to tell her of his undying love, but he finally understands he can never be part of her life. When she leaves, in a burst of hysteria, as suddenly as she arrived, he is left alone in the study of his mother's house and he tears up the manuscript he had been working on before she entered. After he leaves the room we hear a pistol shot and we are told that he has killed himself.

Frances was so moving in the scene that I had no trouble at all being completely involved with her, and I understood fully Trepliov's own sorrow. But what was difficult was the moment when I was alone after she left. What to do? How does one show to the audience you have decided to kill yourself?

We did the scene in class and Frances was even more moving than she had been in rehearsals. And as long as I was on the stage with her I felt secure in what I was doing and feeling, but then came the moment when she left and I was alone, what seemed an eternity, trying somehow to convey, when tearing up the manuscript, that I was making up my mind to kill myself.

When the scene was over Frances and I took our places facing Soloviova and Daykarhanova. They looked at us both for a few minutes and then they turned to each other and began talking in Russian. Madame Soloviova, usually gentle and mild, seemed very agitated and did most of the talking. Madame Daykarhanova lit a cigarette and nodded her head to whatever Soloviova was saying. I stole a look at the other actors in the class. I could see that many of them had been crying. I looked over at Frances. She was watching Madame Soloviova and Daykarhanova intently. Finally they stopped talking and Daykarhanova looked at Frances and shook her head, slowly from side to side.

"Well," she said. "You understand part very, very well. Madame Soloviova has seen it many times at Art Theater and you understand this sad, wretched girl very, very well."

Frances's eyes filled up with tears.

"Thank you, Madame, so much," she said.

"Yes," Madame Daykarhanova said, taking a drag on her cigarette. "You understand her so very well."

Madame Soloviova then talked about the part and how much she felt Frances had accomplished.

Then she and Daykarhanova began talking in Russian again, and again Soloviova did most of the talking. When they finished Daykarhanova lit another cigarette and Soloviova turned to me.

"Very good, what you do, Horton. Very full. Nice quality for Trepliov. Very sympathetic, very . . . " (she searched for a word in English, spoke to Daykarhanova in Russian for help) "Sensitive," Daykarhanova said. "Yes, thank you. Sensitive. Very sensitive. Understand?"

"Yes," I said. "I understand. Thank you. But I don't know what to do after she leaves."

Again the two madames spoke in Russian, and when they finished Soloviova once again turned to me.

"You see. You understand. You do nothing?"

"Nothing?"

"Nothing. All you do is carefully tear up manuscript and put pieces away. Carefully, methodically, as if for last time. You are putting away everything for last time. No hysteria, no emotion, just calmly, methodically for last time and then you leave. Don't worry about emotion," she said. "Just do physical task. Tear up manuscript as if for last time and leave."

Among the students studying with Jilinsky, Daykarhanova, and Soloviova was Mary Hunter. She was in her early thirties, tall, large boned, with dark hair and a handsome face. It was said she had an interest in directing more than in acting, although she did all the exercises diligently.

It was Mary Hunter, with the encouragement of Jilinsky, that began to talk of starting an acting group. I assume it was also discussed with Madame Daykarhanova and Madame Soloviova because in their scene class Mary began to direct Clemence Dane's *Wild December*, a play about the Brontës. Perry Wilson, Mary Virginia Palmer, and Frances Anderson were to be the Brontë sisters, John Forsht, who had returned from Pennsylvania and had begun studying at the studio, their brother. After two months of rehearsal it was shown to Jilinsky, Soloviova, Daykarhanova, and others. Their reaction was very positive and encouraging.

There were rumors then that Mary was going to formally start an acting company and would ask certain of the students at the school to become members.

I was asked to join along with John Forsht and Joe Anthony, and later Lonnie Hinkley, who was studying in another class with Jilinsky. Mary Hunter, as we all expected was to be the director, and Perry Wilson, Betty Goddard, Frances Anderson, Mary Virginia Palmer, Mildred Dunnock, Jane Rose, Lucy Kroll, Fanya Zelinskaya, Patricia Coates, and Beulah Weil were the actresses invited to join. We were to rehearse a play for three months during the summer and then in the fall, if it was worthy, bring it into New York. The plan was to spend the mornings on technique exercises and rehearse the play in the afternoon and part of the evening.

A house was found in Croton-on-Hudson that had been built for Raymond Duncan, Isadora's brother, which had a large studio he had used to teach dance, and was very right for our rehearsals and exercise classes.

Mildred Dunnock and Lucy Kroll rented houses nearby with their husbands, but there were enough rooms in the Duncan house for the rest of us, although four of the girls had to share one very large room and John, Joe, Lonnie, and I had to share another. Mary Hunter and Frances Anderson, who both had husbands coming up for weekends, were given private rooms.

Each of the girls contributed three hundred dollars for the summer, and Joe, too, since he was still in the WPA-funded Federal Theater. Lonnie paid because his family was wealthy. Only John and I were exempt.

On the eighth day we were called together and it was announced by Mary that she, Jilinsky, Madame Daykarhanova, and Madame Soloviova had decided that the play we would rehearse was Edith Hamilton's translation of *The Trojan Women*. The play had been cast by them, too. Mary, of course, was to direct, with the occasional assistance of Jilinsky. Mildred Dunnock was to play Hecuba; Perry Wilson, Cassandra; Frances Anderson, Andromoca; Mary Virginia Palmer, Helen of Troy; Joe Anthony, the Captain; and Lonnie Hinkley, Menelaus. John and I were soldiers, and the rest of the women were to be the chorus. I remember that the last run-through of the play, before we left our house in Croton, was very moving and we were all convinced we would have a great success in New York.

It didn't turn out that way. The reviews were savage. One critic said if Helen of Troy had resembled our Helen there would have been no Trojan War. No one came off well—not the acting, not Mary's direction.

Since John and I had little do in the play we had gotten by

unnoticed. We were puzzled, though, at the savagery of the attacks, frightened, too. I think now if Mary Hunter hadn't had financial resources (she played Marge in the popular radio series *Easy Aces*), and had been as young and immature as most of us, it would have been the last of our company. But fortunately, she had an income and was very determined to continue the work. In the meantime I got a job ushering in a movie house to keep going, John was hired as Mary's secretary, and Joe, besides continuing on the Federal Theater project, began working with Agnes de Mille as her dance partner. Lonnie continued to be supported by his parents and didn't have to work, and neither did any of the girls.

Mary conferred with our teachers and they decided that the choice of our first play was a mistake for such a young company. Then she had the idea that since we called ourselves the American Actors Company, we would only do American plays.

Mary had lived her teenage years in New Mexico with her aunt, the novelist Mary Austen. There she had met the then very young playwright Lynn Riggs and they became devoted friends. The Theater Guild had done Lynn Riggs's play *Green Grow the Lilacs* with Franchot Tone and June Walker a few seasons earlier. The play was a critical success but made no money, and few of his plays had since been done in New York. He was now living in the city and Mary went to him and asked if he would let us produce one of his plays. He came to the studio to meet with us, and I suppose, though I don't remember, to see something of our work. He agreed to give us his play *Sump'n Like Wings.* Paul Green had had a similar experience with his play *The House of Connelly,* produced by the Group Theater, and had no successful play in New

York since then. He was a friend of Lynn's and Lynn approached him about giving us a play, too, and he agreed. It was *Shroud My Body Down.*

We rented space over a garage, which was large enough to have a small stage at one end and at the other to seat thirty people. We called it our studio.

After four weeks of rehearsal we opened *Sump'n Like Wings,* and critics were invited. None of them came, but the play and the production were enthusiastically received by the audiences. Agnes de Mille came, and James T. Farrell, Lynn, of course, and a young playwright friend of his, Ramon Naya, Paul Green, and many other theater people. Lynn was very happy with the production. Ramon Naya had two plays, *Empire in Durango* and *Mexican Mural,* which he gave to Mary to read in hopes that we would one day produce them.

Arnold Sundgaard, another young playwright, saw the production and said he would like to work with us, too.

That spring we began rehearsing some one-act plays. Mary was to direct, and I was cast, along with Joe Anthony, and John Forsht in E. P. Conkle's *Minnie Field.* There were also two other one-act plays, both by Paul Green.

Again, no theater critics came, but we had full houses and there was enthusiasm from the audiences. John Martin, the dance critic for *The New York Times,* attended and was very impressed. He gave us a one-act play, which he hoped we would one day produce.

The American Actors Company disbanded for the summer and I got a job acting at the Maverick Theater in Woodstock, New York, where I was to play Mio in Maxwell Anderson's *Win-*

terset and Mister Mister in Marc Blitzstein's *The Cradle Will Rock*.
I had seen *Winterset* in 1936 when it played at the Martin Beck
Theater with Burgess Meredith and Margo. The play, in verse,
takes place in a time after the Sacco and Vanzetti trials and exam-
ines the effect the execution of Vanzetti has on his son. Mr.
Meredith brought a kind of cocky bravado to the part of Mio, and
made terrifying his rage over the injustice done his father. He
was moving and heartbreaking in his grief over his father's death.
Every young male actor I knew in New York coveted the part and
wanted somehow to get a chance to play it. Not only was the part
emotionally and physically demanding, but there were a great
number of lines to learn, all in verse. Fortunately, in Woodstock
we had a talented company that worked well together and I
enjoyed the whole experience very much.

CHAPTER 9

*Mary Hunter Wolf, Joseph Anthony,
and Horton Foote*

The political climate in New York at the time was radically different from anything I had known in Texas or Pasadena. The politics I heard discussed by the men in my father's store could become violent and extreme at times, but they had to do either with the personalities of the competing candidates, or what they felt was good for the South and its cotton economy. In Pasadena the Depression was never mentioned and I heard nothing of politics of any kind, but in New York City I was soon assailed on every side with the politics of change. I became conscious for the first time of the enormity of the Depression and learned that young men and women that I liked and admired felt Roosevelt was not doing enough to help the poor. Now these were not the old Mossback Roosevelt haters of my Texas days, but bright, talented young people, and I heard from them the words *Communist* and *Socialist* spoken as casually as in Texas we had said *Republican* and *Democrat*. I heard about labor unions and my responsibility to become politically active. I was invited to parties where politics were discussed and argued by people my age. I was invited to march in many parades and I did so quite happily, shouting as loud as I could with the rest, "Wages up and prices down! Make New York a Union town!"

I became aware of Nazis and Fascists and began, as was the fashion then, to call anyone I suspected of right leanings a Fascist. I was invited to attend a Communist cell with friends and went and found here a group of very average Americans along with some famous theater people; it was all very earnest, and on the whole very low key. It reminded me somewhat of the Epworth League meetings for young people that I had attended back home at the Methodist church.

There was one puzzling moment, though, when a well-known modern dance choreographer, a contemporary of Martha Graham, stood up and said she had long ago seen the seeds of fascism in Martha Graham's dancing, and I was surprised when no one challenged her. I thought, going home, that maybe she was right—maybe I had missed something. I had already seen Martha Graham dance, and though I knew little about dance of any kind, certainly not modern dance, I had been struck by the extraordinary force of her dancing and choreography. I couldn't wait to see her dance again. She appeared rarely in those days because she couldn't afford to rent a theater, but when she finally did I was there, and felt her critic at the cell meeting crazy.

Then Mary Hunter heard of my interests and called me to her apartment for a talk. She told me that her husband, Jack Sullivan, was working with the American Labor Party and that they were very active in progressive politics, but were anti-Communist, and felt I should be very careful, and thoughtful, before aligning with anyone. I thanked her and said I would be. Later at her apartment I often met James T. Farrell, who was very popular at the time because of his novels. His friends were all passionately pro-Labor but anti-Communist. I began reading *Partisan Review* and read of Trotsky and the charges of his murder by the Stalinists in Mexico. Finally, one day Jilinsky spoke of his reason for leaving the Soviet Union. It was because of Stalin, he said, and that he was a murderer and a tyrant. It did impress me to hear him speak so passionately and bitterly, but he never, that I knew of, spoke that way again.

On my next visit to Texas I couldn't wait to share my new knowledge of politics with my parents.

The six cotton farms owned by my grandmother, which my father managed, were all worked by black sharecroppers. The injustices of the Cotton South were very much on the mind of my liberal friends, and the miseries of the tenant farmers, black or white, were endlessly discussed by them.

The first night I was home, as we sat under the chinaberry trees in the backyard, my mother began asking me questions about Madame Daykarhanova and her school, and my classmates. My father asked me how much I was making at my various jobs, which wasn't much, God knows, but enough to convince him that I was making some kind of a living. I answered all their questions patiently and then began a diatribe on the unfairness of the tenant system, and the exploitation of blacks in the South.

My parents listened patiently as I became more and more agitated, but when I paused to take a breath, my father asked: "I hope you're still a Democrat, son?"

"Yes," I said. "I'm still a Democrat."

"I tell you, son," he said sounding relieved, "I could forgive you almost anything except your voting the Republican ticket."

"We're having a time here now, son," my mother said.

"What about?" I asked.

"Honey," she said, sounding really alarmed, "half our family aren't speaking. It's just terrible."

"Why?" I asked.

My father answered, "Because they're ungrateful. They're Roosevelt haters. Half of my relatives, God help me, are Roosevelt haters. I just don't get it after all he's done for the South."

"Who hates Roosevelt?"

"Thomas Abell is the leader of the pack here. Sister's husband Will Coffee voted Republican on the last election."

"How do you know?"

"Because he drove all the way from Houston Sunday a week ago to tell me. Sister sitting right beside him as he bragged about it. And I said, 'Sister, did you vote Republican, too?' 'I did,' she said, just as smug as you please. Why in the name of God," my father almost shouting now.

"Now, honey," my mother said. "Don't get all worked up."

"I'm sorry, hon," he said, "but I am worked up. The very thought of the two of them riding all the way from Houston to tell me that just infuriates me."

"Did you ask her why she voted Republican?"

"Yes, I did."

"And what did she say?"

"She said because of Mrs. Roosevelt."

"Mrs. Roosevelt?"

"Yes. She said she had gotten the Negroes in Houston starting Disappointment Clubs."

"What are they?"

"She says you read in the papers want ads of a colored woman applying for a job as a maid or a cook and you call them to come for an interview and they come and you make arrangements to hire them, you agree on a salary and the day for them to start work, and then when that day comes they don't show up, which means they are members of the Disappointment Clubs whose purpose is to disappoint white ladies. 'And you believe that foolishness,' I asked her? 'Of course, I do,' she said. 'I know it as a fact. It's happened to all my friends.' 'All your friends,' I said. 'Well, a number of them, hasn't it, Will?' And you know what Will said? 'I'm sorry to say it has.' 'I wouldn't put anything past the Roosevelts. She just hates the South,' Sister said, 'she is taking out all her unhappiness on the South.' I tell you, it was all I could do not to throw them out of my house."

"Is Thomas Abell a Republican, too?" I asked.

"No, he's worse," he said. "He's a Dixiecrat. Have you heard about them?"

"Yes."

"Well, they're about to take over the Democratic Party here, and last week we went to a caucus meeting here at the courthouse, and Thomas and his cohorts began their shenanigans to try and take over the party caucus. And our cousin Junior Hawes, who is the leader of the loyal Democrats, said we shouldn't stay and watch them practice their deceit and he told all the loyal Democrats to leave with him and we could have our own meeting and that's what we did. And you know what those Dixiecrats did? They hissed us as we left."

That night in bed I thought of all I'd say to my cousin Thomas Abell, and my uncle Will Coffee when I met them, but the next day Aunt Lyda, Thomas's mother, called my mother to ask us all for supper the next day, and said Thomas and his family would be there, too. My mother accepted, but she said later she wouldn't go unless my daddy and I promised not to discuss politics.

"What if Thomas brings it up?" I asked.

"Well, don't respond. Just find a way to change the subject. Talk about New York," my mother said. "Now promise me."

"I promise," I said.

And Daddy promised her that. And maybe someone had made Thomas promise that, too, because politics was not mentioned once.

I stayed home most of this visit, reading in the daytime and sitting on the front porch with my father and mother at night, or in the backyard listening to the music, blues mostly, coming from the Negro barbecue restaurant in the Flats. It was August and the evenings were warm, but every now and then a breeze from the Gulf cooled things off. My mother tried to keep the conversation about my life in New York, and my father would join her in questioning for a while, and then sensing what he really wanted to talk about was politics, I would start him off by asking about the cousins who were good Democrats and those that were, in his eyes, renegades. My visit lasted until I felt the time had come for me to say good-bye again and get back to New York to look for work.

CHAPTER 10

Franchot Tone

One of the producers of the Maverick Theater spoke to me as the summer there was ending. He was going to be associated with a production of one-act plays in the fall. He said he would call me when we got back to New York and arrange for me to meet the director, Em. Joe Bashee. He and Bashee were producing the plays with William Kozlenko, editor and publisher of *The One Act Play Magazine.* We had all promised when joining the American Actors Company to be available for productions no matter what we were offered by other theaters. When I got back to New York I called Mary Hunter, who had now become our authority in all matters relating to the company, and asked what should I do. She said wait until you get the offer and we'll know by then more definitely what our plans are.

The One Act Repertory Theater cast me in two of the plays—*The Coggerers* by Paul Vincent Carroll, one of Ireland's leading playwrights in the 1930s, and *The Red Velvet Goat* by Josephina Niggli. I immediately called Mary and she said go ahead, since our next production wouldn't began rehearsals until late winter.

The One Act Repertory Theater was to open at the Hudson Theater in the late fall, with a cast of well-known Broadway actors. That's how we designated people in those days, at least I did—he's a Broadway actor, or he's never been on Broadway, or he's making his Broadway debut. The latter was what I was doing, of course, and I could hardly believe that this was finally happening after five long years.

Paul Vincent Carroll's play takes place in a Dublin museum where statues of Irish patriots come to life and speak to a cleaning woman. I played Robert Emmet, who had been hanged, drawn, and quartered by his enemies. I was in period costume, prehanging of course, and all of us, the statues, had special makeups to give our faces a proper look.

Josephina Niggli, the author of *The Red Velvet Goat,* was Mexican, and a cousin of Ramon Naya's. She had studied playwriting at the University of North Carolina with Paul Green. I played a sixteen-year-old Mexican boy in her play.

Rehearsals went very well. All of us, the actors, were fond of the director, Em. Joe Bashee, and each other. We were warned that one-act plays had never found any kind of an audience in New York. But this time, because of the plays and the actors, the producers felt it might be different.

It wasn't. Brooks Atkinson wrote:

Mr. Carroll's drama has a vivid setting. To put the Easter Monday rebellion into an Irish nationalistic perspective he stages his drama in the entrance hall of a Dublin library, where the white statues of Irish heroes and martyrs stand on their pedestals or look out of their niches. To most people they are cold marble statues. But they are on familiar terms with the slatternly old charwoman who dusts them. When the rebellion breaks out in the streets her only son is one of the first victims, and, abetted by a stirring, deeply affecting performance by Irene Oshiar, Mr. Carroll's play shows how the heroes and martyrs of Ireland comfort the mother of a fresh, young hero and receive him into their august company. Even "The Coggerers" is a little too long for its dramatic impact, but is the one play of the evening with an original idea, professional skill in the writing and acting.

We closed after five performances.

I was heartbroken but found little sympathy from my fellow members of the American Actors Company. They said I should know by now what the Broadway system was like, and that instead of mourning, I should put all of my energy in making our company a success, since it was companies like ours that were to be the salvation of the American theater.

In 1939, the New York World's Fair was scheduled to open at Flushing Meadows. There was to be a spectacle, "Railroads on Parade." It was to be a celebration of the railroads of America, their history, and a prophecy of their future. They built a special arena for the show and hired an enormous company of actors and dancers. I don't believe the director, Charles Allen, had ever directed before and to my knowledge never directed again. Bill Matons, a promising young choreographer, was to choreograph. I would have a job in the late spring.

* * *

Mary Hunter had an idea for a kind of folk revue with dancing, singing, and some sketches she would call *American Legend.* She had asked Agnes de Mille to choreograph the dances and to work with her in finding a form for the whole. It was to be ready for the 1940–41 season. We were also working on another series of one-act plays. Before starting rehearsals for the one acts, we worked with Agnes and Mary on a series of improvisations. Since we were all from different parts of the country, Mary suggested that each of us perform an improvisation based on our particular region.

I did five improvisations about Texas and after one of them, Agnes called me over and asked, "Have you ever thought about writing?"

"No," I said.

"Have you never written?" she asked.

"Well, when I was a junior in high school I wrote a short story for a cousin who was failing English at Texas University."

Many years later I read that Charles Ives's father, George, told him when he was beginning to write music: "If a poet knows more about a horse than he does about heaven, he might better stick to the horse, and someday the horse might carry him into heaven."

When Agnes suggested I write a play, I asked, "What shall I write about?" She put it more bluntly than Charles Ives's father. "Write about what you know," she said.

I went home that night to my West Side room and wrote a one-act play. It was based, as the improvisations had been based, on an event, partly real, partly imagined. I used names of real people, and wrote the lead for myself. I wrote one draft and took it back to the company and told Mary Hunter what I had done. She asked to read it. She took it home and came back the next day and said she wanted to do it with the other one-act plays in the spring.

I called the play *Wharton Dance* and it was done with two one-act plays by Thornton Wilder. Robert Coleman of the *Mirror* was the first of the New York critics to come to our productions. He came opening night and the next day he reviewed the plays. He was impressed with my play, praised Mary's direction, and liked all the actors, giving me a special mention.

As soon as the plays closed, rehearsals began for "Railroads on Parade." It was indeed a spectacle. Horses, wagons, trains, bicycles, cowboys, Indians, Chinese peasants. We gave three shows a day and most of us were in eight scenes during a show, which meant changing clothes twenty-four times.

I met Valerie Bettis, who later was to play such an important part in my life. She was one of the dancers and I didn't like her very much. I thought she was affected and stuck-up. Betty Garrett, who later was featured in many MGM musicals, was one of the dancers, too. I liked her a great deal, and so did every other male in the company. We all competed for her attention.

The men dressed in one huge room and the women in another. It was one of the few times in that day that blacks and whites appeared in the same show and dressed together. New York was then still very segregated. In the fall, "Railroads on Parade" closed for the season, promising to reopen in the spring.

I now shared an apartment with five other actors and a playwright. Mary Virginia Palmer, Joe Anthony, Frances Reid, Bea

Newport, Philip Bourneuf were the actors and Philip Lewis, the playwright.

Frances Reid and Bea Newport were both from the Pasadena Playhouse and Philip Bourneuf was a member of the Alfred Lunt–Lynn Fontanne Company, which was at present on hiatus. Philip Lewis was an unproduced playwright, with several plays under option. He also looked for acting jobs that would support his playwrighting and had been hired by the Theater Guild for a small part in Ernest Hemingway's *The Fifth Column.* He said there were other small parts available and that I should look into it.

I went to the Guild office the next day but I was told by the receptionist that it was all cast.

That Friday I went out to Jackson Heights to spend the weekend with Perry Wilson and her family. We were up fairly early Saturday morning and having breakfast when the phone rang. Perry answered and said it was for me. It was Philip Lewis. He was calling from the *Fifth Column* rehearsal and said an actor had left. He had spoken to the stage manager about me, and I should get into town as soon as possible and go directly to the theater. I arrived while the company was on lunch break. The doorman told me to wait while he went for the stage manager. Philip Lewis came by then and told me I was to meet the director.

"Who is the director?" I asked.

"Lee Strasberg. We have a first-rate company. Franchot Tone, Lee J. Cobb, Lenore Ulric, and Katherine Locke." The stage manager came in then and Philip introduced us and I followed the stage manager onto the stage where Strasberg and Franchot Tone were talking. The stage manager took me up to them, but they kept on talking until finally he said, "Mr. Strasberg, the actor you wanted to see is here." Strasberg stopped then and looked up at me.

"What's your name?" Strasberg asked in that impersonal tone he often used.

"Horton Foote," I said, not feeling nervous at all, which surprised me greatly.

Strasberg's expression didn't change as he continued to look at me.

"Have you trained anyplace?"

"What do you mean, sir?"

"He means have you studied acting with anyone?" Franchot Tone said and gave me what I thought was an encouraging smile.

"Yessir."

"Where?" Strasberg said, his expression still not changing.

"Daykarhanova's School for the Stage," I said. "I did scenes in her class. Also for Madame Soloviova, and I studied technique with Jilinsky."

"I saw Daykarhanova in Balieff's *Chauve Souris,*" Franchot Tone said.

"Jilinsky and Soloviova came here with Michael Chekhov's company. She was the queen in *Hamlet.* She was very good, too. I forgot what Jilinsky played," Strasberg said.

Again, he looked me over, then he turned to Franchot Tone. "Okay, Franchot?"

"Okay with me," Franchot said.

"Paul?" he called and the stage manager appeared. "Give him his sides and have him wait in the theater. I won't get to him today, but he should be watching."

I followed the stage manager into the theater auditorium and he told me to take a seat anywhere. Philip Lewis came in then with Wendell Phillips, a slight, thin man with a worried expression, and an actor in the company. He introduced us and then asked the stage manager what had happened, and the stage manager said I had the part.

"Did you read for him?" Philip asked me.

"No, he didn't ask me to. He just asked me who I studied with, and I told him."

"Who did you study with?" Wendell asked.

"Daykarhanova, Jilinsky, and Soloviova," I said.

"Lee studied at the Actor's Lab with Ouspenskaya and Boleslavsky. Lee is a great teacher, too, you know," Wendell said. "He was my teacher. He taught me everything I know."

The stage manager came back with my sides and handed them to me.

"I forgot to ask, are you a member of Equity?"

"Yessir, I joined last year when I was in the One Act Repertory Theater."

"Fine," he said and left.

"What's my part like?" I asked Philip.

"You have one scene. The play takes place in Spain during the civil war. You have been arrested falsely on a spy charge and you're brought in and questioned and you're very scared."

The other actors begin to come into the theater, laughing and talking.

"Which one is Lenore Ulric?" I asked.

"There she is," Philip said, pointing to a middle-aged lady, swarthy skin, black hair worn shoulder length; she seemed tense and nervous. She was wearing a very short, tight-fitting skirt and blouse and she sat in a corner of the theater by herself.

"I'm sorry," Philip said, "I'm old-fashioned, I guess, but I don't think you ask a star like Miss Ulric to sit in the theater with the rest of us and wait until she's needed. She should be in her dressing room and sent for."

Lee J. Cobb came in and said hello as he passed us on his way to the stage. He looked the same to me as he'd looked in Pasadena.

"He's going to be very good in this," Wendell said.

"I saw him do Herod in *Salome* at the Pasadena Playhouse and he was wonderful," I said.

Katherine Locke came in then and she walked over to Philip and Wendell. She was simply, almost severely dressed, and wearing no makeup. You had to look closely to see how lovely she really was.

"Katherine," Philip said. "This is Horton Foote. He's going to be with us."

"Fine," she said, "Welcome."

"Thank you," I said. She walked over to Lee Cobb and they began talking.

I had seen her in *Wish You Were Here* with John Garfield. I had liked her a great deal and wanted to tell her so, but I wasn't sure if that's what professionals did, so I kept quiet. I looked over at her then, talking to Lee Cobb and I thought she was really very, very attractive, with a quiet kind of beauty and sweetness.

Philip Lewis and I left rehearsals together at five o'clock and took the subway to our apartment. I still couldn't believe what had happened and just before we went down to the subway I said for the tenth time, "Philip. Thank you again for thinking of me."

"I'm glad it worked out. I only hope the play runs a long time and we'll have jobs for the whole season."

Rehearsals began the next day at ten. Philip and I took the subway uptown together to the Guild Theater. I had learned my part and wondered if Strasberg would get to my scene that day. I was going to ask Philip if he thought he would, but the subway was noisy and crowded and I decided to wait and ask the question when we were back on the street, but coming out of the subway we met Wendell Phillips and he began talking about Strasberg again as we walked toward the theater.

"Once he had me so upset and insecure in class that I couldn't eat and I couldn't sleep. Finally, I went to him and I said, 'Lee, you have to tell me this. Am I without talent? Don't lie to me. Am I without talent?' "

"What did he say?" I asked.

"Not much. You know he doesn't talk much. He just said, 'If you were without talent I would have told you. I would have said, "Don't waste my time. Don't waste your time."' "

Miss Ulric was in the theater when we got there.

"I hope he uses her today," Philip said. "He made her stay here all yesterday and he never used her once. He has no consideration."

"He just focuses on the work. He has no time for consideration," Wendell said.

The other actors arrived. Franchot Tone last of all. The stage manager announced the schedule of scenes and rehearsals began. The scene went on for a few moments, when Lee stopped and called to the stage manager to ask Miss Ulric to come onstage.

She must have heard Lee, because she got up before the stage manager spoke to her. She seemed to me like a racehorse at the starting gate.

"She was a great star, you know," Philip said to me.

"A long time ago," Wendell said.

"Not that long ago," Philip replied.

"Did you ever see her perform?" I asked.

"No," Philip said.

"No," Wendell said. "She was a Belasco star."

"I read once she was in *Kiki* and *Lulu Belle.* What else?" I asked.

"I don't remember," Philip said.

"I hear she's broke now," Wendell said.

"I wonder what they're paying her for this?" Philip said.

"You know the Guild. She's not getting rich on this, I can tell you," Wendell said. "I'm working for minimum."

The stage manager called out into the auditorium, "Let's have it quiet, please."

Wendell and Philip stopped talking then and I saw Miss Ulric walk offstage for a moment and then reenter, almost running. She was a force, all right, controlled, but again I thought of a racehorse. She said a few lines and Strasberg stopped her. He went over to her and said something but so quietly that I couldn't hear him.

Late in the afternoon I was called onstage and the stage manager showed me where I was to go.

Strasberg went out into the auditorium to watch and I could see Miss Ulric watching, too, from offstage. We began the scene, and continued on to the end. The other actors in the scene went down to the footlights as if expecting Strasberg to say something. All he said was, "Next scene please." The stage manager came onstage to rearrange some props. As he passed me he said, "Okay."

I went into the auditorium over to Wendell and Philip.

"Good," Philip said.

"Strasberg didn't say anything," I said.

"Don't worry about that," Wendell said. "That's just how he is. He only tells you if he's not pleased. He's very complicated. In my opinion a genius, but very, very complicated."

We had a run-through of the play on the stage of the Guild just before leaving for New Haven. The actors weren't allowed in the theater, but had to stay in the dressing rooms until it was time for our entrance onstage, so none of us had any idea how it went. We knew that out front were the Guild Board, Lawrence Langner, Theresa Helburn, and Armina Marshall. Philip said Billy Rose, who was coproducing the play, was there, too. When the run-through was finished, the stage manager called the company onstage and thanked us, and said we would get any notes from Strasberg at rehearsal in New Haven, and that he would see us at Grand Central Station at ten in the morning. Wendell walked to the subway with me and Philip.

"You were right, Philip," Wendell said. "Billy Rose was out there watching."

"What a strange combination," Philip said. "The Theater Guild, the producers of O'Neill and Shaw, and Billy Rose. A tough, tough show man."

"He brings the money, I guess," Wendell said. "He is tough, you know, and very opinionated. I hope he doesn't cause trouble."

*   *   *

Wendell sat beside me on the train to New Haven. I began to ask him questions about his work with the Group Theater. I knew that Strasberg and Cheryl Crawford had left and I asked him why. He didn't seem to want to talk about that, but constantly returned to Lee and the debt he felt he owed him, and how much the Group owed him. He then began to talk about the approaches to acting that he thought had caused the final separation. Issues I've heard discussed, pro and con, now through the years. What Stella Adler feels and what Harold Clurman feels and what Lee Strasberg feels and who is right, but it was all new to me then, and I kept asking him more and more questions. He asked me about Jilinsky's teaching and I tried to explain what little I felt I understood of it. I remember his asking me how we used affective memory in his classes and I stuttered and stumbled around. I finally confessed that if I had heard Jilinsky use the term, I had forgotten it. Then he explained in fascinating detail Lee Strasberg's approach to the use of it, and said that it was the use of affective memory that Stella Adler most violently opposed in his work.

Just before the dress rehearsal started in New Haven, you could feel the tension growing in the company. Even Katherine Locke, usually so serene and calm, seemed tense and nervous. When I passed her backstage and wished her luck, she gave me a sickly smile and said nothing. I wanted to find Miss Ulric and wish her luck, but when I asked the stage manager where her dressing room was he told me to stay away as she was very nervous and didn't want to talk to anyone. I had talked to Lee Cobb earlier in rehearsal and told him how much I liked him in *Salome* back in Pasadena, and he seemed pleased and astounded that anyone in the East had seen it. Franchot Tone I avoided like the plague, because he seemed moody and imperious.

Many, many years later in 1960, Franchot played Mark Twain in *The Shape of the River*, a television play I wrote for Playhouse 90. I had seen his brilliant work as Astrov in Stark Young's translation of Chekhov's *Uncle Vanya*, and I knew Stark Young regarded him as one of our finest actors. I was impressed by how hard he worked during the rehearsals of *The Shape of the River* and how anxious he was to get it all right, and splendid he was, too. During rehearsals we became friends and unlike so many friendships developed in rehearsals ours continued until his death.

I was sharing a dressing room with Philip, Wendell, and three other actors. My scene wasn't until the second act, but I was told by the stage manager to stay in the dressing room until it was time for me to go onstage. I had no idea how the play was going, and was dependent on the reports from the other actors as they came back to the dressing room to change clothes. I was told, though, Billy Rose was again out front for the dress rehearsal.

It was the same for opening night in New Haven. I was banished to my dressing room, but I was told both nights had gone well.

The morning after, the stage manager asked us all to gather in the theater. Katherine and Franchot weren't there, but Miss Ulric was sitting alone as usual. I sat next to Philip and Wendell.

Lee Strasberg asked the stage manager to call the company closer together. He did so and we all moved down front. Strasberg said he had been basically pleased, but certain weaknesses in the play had become obvious with an audience there. Trims had to be made, certain scenes rewritten, and some of the staging rethought. We rehearsed every day, except for matinees. I was allowed in the theater during rehearsals, but couldn't tell if the changes were any good or not, or why they were even made. My scene wasn't touched and I breathed a sigh of relief. We opened in Philadelphia on a Tuesday and again I had to depend on reports from the other actors about the show. They felt on the whole it had improved, and said we'll see in the morning what the critics say.

Philip, who said he had had a nervous stomach all his life, wondered why anyone with a nervous stomach would choose the theater as a profession where you had to wait and see what critics would say to know if you had a job or not.

"Do you have a nervous stomach now?" I asked.

"I certainly do. The worst I've ever had."

Wednesday morning I was in Philip's room at the hotel when there was a knock at the door and I opened it and Wendell was there with the morning papers. He didn't look very happy.

"Are they bad?" Philip asked despondently.

"Not bad. Just disappointing. They say we need work. We're too long."

"What did they say about Franchot?"

"All right for him."

"And Katherine?"

"So. So."

"And Miss Ulric?" I asked.

"Said she seemed not always sure. They said she had once been a big Belasco star, and this was her debut as a featured player."

*   *   *

The next two weeks in Philadelphia were hectic. Changes every day. One scene was cut out entirely. The actors were irritable and tired. What had been a fairly harmonious company had now become depressed and very tense.

On Friday night of the second week the stage manager came up to my dressing room and asked to talk to me out in the hall. I followed him outside.

"I have some bad news for you," he said. "You won't be going to Boston with us. They're cutting your scene out of the play. Strasberg says to thank you and it has nothing to do with your acting. He thinks you're very good, it's just the scene seems to be extraneous now."

"Yessir," I said. "Thank you."

"Sure," he said and went down the stairs.

Philip and Wendell were waiting as I came back into the dressing room.

"What's that about?" Philip asked.

"They're cutting my scene out of the play," I said.

"I'm sorry. I'm sorry. I'm sorry," Wendell said, and I knew he meant it.

"I hate this lousy business," Philip said. "I just hate it."

I rode the train with them Sunday morning until we got to New York. Then I told them good-bye and got off the train.

The Fifth Column was not a critical success, although on the strength of Franchot Tone's name it ran for a while. Lenore Ulric appeared some years later with Katharine Cornell in *Anthony and Cleopatra,* then disappeared from the New York stage. She died at seventy-eight in the Rockland State Hospital where she had been for a number of years. I was told that none of the other patients knew what she had done in the theater. One day the film *Camille* with Greta Garbo, in which she had played a supporting role, was shown to the patients. When her face appeared on the screen she said to those around her, "Look, that's me," but no one believed her.

In the late spring rehearsals began again for "Railroads on Parade." England was in the midst of the Blitz and there were very divided feelings in the company about our role in all this. I was pro-Allied Forces, as were most of my friends, but there were others that were equally passionate about our staying out of the war.

I saved as much money as I could and when the show closed late fall, I decided to go to Wharton to try to write a three-act play. A week later I took a train coach to Houston, sitting up all night thinking of possible ideas.

So much had changed since my last visit home. My brother Tom Brooks was now in college. He, too, wanted to be an actor, but my father had convinced him to go first to college and get a degree before going to New York. I had gotten to know Hazel Strayer, the head of the drama department at an Iowa college, and I suggested that he study with her. The tuition was modest, and my father thought it an excellent suggestion, so my brother had left for Iowa a month before my arrival.

It had nearly been seven years since I left Wharton for Pasadena, and as always on my return trips I went over in my mind a kind of inner inventory. On the positive side I knew I could now support myself in New York City, no matter how modestly. I felt I had the right to now call myself an actor, and that with continuing hard work and training I might in time be a very good actor. Still, in all fairness, my acting résumé was extremely modest, and there was no recognition at all from the people at home when I told them the plays I had been in.

My cousin Nannie met me again at the train station in Houston. She had always been supportive of my desire to be an actor, and I never doubted her loyalty to me, but I also felt she would be disappointed unless I was going to play the lead in a Broadway play or star in a film. She pretended always to be interested in what I was doing, but the pageants and the small, obscure off-Broadway theaters must have had little meaning for her, or indeed for anyone else in my family or among my Wharton friends. They were mostly good actors, though, and hid their disappointment.

Seven years had also brought about many changes in Wharton—deaths of relatives and old family friends, my grandmother moving to Houston, her house now occupied by renters. The wear I could see in the faces of my great aunts, uncles, cousins, and my mother and father as they grew older always affected me greatly. I sometimes thought about staying and never leaving again. What if I went down to my father's store and said to him, I'm here to stay now and to repaint the store sign to read *Al. H. Foote & Son,* as if my staying could somehow stop the changes. Such fantasies, however, didn't last long, because for good or bad, I knew that in a month or so I would get restless and need to return to New York City.

Nannie had read my one-act play, *Wharton Dance,* and spent

most of the drive back telling me who she thought the characters were based on. When I finally got her away from talking about the play and onto news of my family and the town, she prefaced every remark by saying, "Now, don't you dare put what I'm telling you in a play."

My mother had Catherine, our cook, prepare a meal for me that included all of my favorite dishes—fried chicken, rice, gravy, mustard greens, biscuits, small, light, and crisp, the way I liked them, fried corn, salad, and pecan pie for dessert.

They asked me a few questions about New York and my work, and then my father was off on the war in Europe and what a tragedy it would be if England were defeated. My mother interrupted him finally to ask how long would I stay this visit.

"I don't know, Mother," I said. "As long as it takes me to write a new play. Maybe a month, maybe two months. I don't know."

"Wouldn't it be wonderful if it were two months," she said.

"I have to work hard," I said. "There can't be a lot of visiting."

"That's all right," she said. "People will understand if you're busy writing a play. Won't they, hon?"

"I think so," my father said.

"You will go and see Aunt Loula and Aunt Lyda, though," Mother said, "and let them have you over for at least one meal. And Mama will want to come visit, I'm sure, for a few days."

"I would want her to," I said. "And I want to see my aunts. How does Tom Brooks like Iowa?" I asked.

My father sighed and shook his head and his face had a grim look almost of despair.

"Now, hon," my mother said. "It still may work out."

"I don't know," he said. "He's stubborn and willful."

"What's wrong?" I asked.

"He doesn't like it," my father said. "He has to learn, you know, that money doesn't grow on trees. You just can't turn around every five minutes and come up with money."

"Now, hon, calm down," my mother said.

"He wants to leave and go to New York with you. I hope you'll talk some sense into him," my father said.

I finished the play in five weeks. I called Mary and told her. She asked, "Would you send me a copy right away?" and I said, "I can't because it's in my handwriting and I only have one copy."

"Oh, Horton," she said, "when are you coming back?"

"I'll leave tomorrow," I said.

After I finished talking to Mary I went down to my father's store, where my mother was visiting.

"I've got news for you," I said. "I've finished my play."

"Oh, that's wonderful, son," my mother said. "Isn't that wonderful, hon?"

"It sure is," my father said. "When can we read it?"

"It's in my handwriting still," I said.

"Merciful God," he said. "When are you going to have it typed up?"

"When I get back to New York," I said.

"When will that be?" he said.

"I want to leave in the morning."

"What's the play called, son?" my mother asked.

"Texas Town," I said.

"Well, I'm happy for you, son," she said, "but I was hoping you'd be here at least two months."

"Well, he has work to do, hon," my father said. "I understand his going."

I wanted for a moment to embrace both of them and tell them how much I loved them, and that I would give up plays and acting and stay here with them. But I knew in my heart that no matter what happened to me in New York, my life in Wharton would be a series of hellos and good-byes from now on, and I knew they knew it, too.

CHAPTER 11

Arnold Sundgaard   *Tennessee Williams*

As soon as I got back to New York I phoned Mary and she told me to take the play to a typing service right away and have six copies made and the company would pay for it.

I found a typing service on Forty-second Street and I showed the manager of the service what I wanted typed. She shook her head as she began to read the script, and after a few minutes she sighed and turned back to me.

"This is going to cost more than we usually charge. Your handwriting is very difficult to read," she said.

Mary had me over for dinner that night. Her husband, Jack Sullivan, was there and Lynn Riggs and Ramon Naya. Lynn, in his late thirties, his sandy hair thinning, wore thick-lensed glasses. Ramon Naya was extremely handsome, and I was told later that he was from a wealthy, aristocratic Mexican family that didn't approve of his being a playwright and refused to support him.

I knew Lynn was to have a play done on Broadway in the fall and had asked the company for permission to use Perry Wilson as one of the leads. The company had said yes, and I was happy for Perry, but disappointed, too, because I wanted her for *Texas Town*. Earlier Mary had told me we couldn't do my play until the spring, because Katherine Dunham was in town from Chicago with her group of dancers for a series of Sunday night performances that Mary was to direct.

"Joe Anthony told me," I said, "that he and Agnes de Mille will be giving a dance recital at the YMHA in the fall."

"Yes," Mary said. "Agnes has been working very hard and she has a whole new program."

"Have you seen her new works?" Lynn asked.

"Yes, I have," Mary said. "It's some of her best work."

"How is Joe?" Ramon asked.

"He's wonderful," Mary said, laughing at the thought of it.

"Agnes," she continued, "does four solos, and then they do two numbers together. You know, he's a wonderful actor and what he lacks in technique as a dancer he makes up for with his acting."

"I tell you," Jack said, "when Katherine Dunham does her Sunday shows this winter, she's going to create a sensation. Wait until you see her."

"And she's discovered two wonderful male dancers," Mary said. "Archie Savage and Tally Beatty. Just wonderful, and her husband, John Pratt, has costumed her brilliantly and has stunning ideas for the sets."

"He's white, you know," Jack said.

"What difference does that make, Jack?" Mary asked.

"It makes no difference. I just think it's interesting."

"You saw her dance in Chicago?" Ramon said.

"Many times," Jack said. "She's something else. She and Mary are very close friends."

"Agnes told me," Lynn said, "that there's talk of starting a new ballet company, and they've asked her to think of a ballet for them."

"They have," Mary said. "Lucia Chase is backing it and, they would like, I understand, to use as many Americans as possible for the company."

"Why did Agnes leave England?" Ramon asked.

"Well," Mary said, "she saw the war coming, of course, and I don't know. Anyway, I think she learned a great deal. She said she worked with two extraordinary dancers over there, Anthony Tudor and Hugh Laing. And they're anxious to come to America, and she hopes if this ballet company materializes, they will be part of it."

"What's happening with *American Legend*?" I asked.

"We've done some work on it," Mary said. "It's coming along slowly. The Humphrey-Weidman Studio Theater would be available to us, and we'd have to do it in a space like that. Our studio is too small."

"Where is the Humphrey-Weidman Studio?" I asked.

"It's on Sixteenth Street," Mary said. "The dancers Doris Humphrey and Charles Weidman teach classes there and give performances twice a year."

"Would you do *American Legend* before Horton's play or afterward?" Jack asked.

"We'd do Horton's play first, if we think it's ready," Mary said.

"Have you read it yet?" Ramon asked.

"No," Mary said. "It's being typed now."

"You'll have it in three days," I said.

"Good," Mary said.

"Mary," Ramon said. "Lynn told me you and Agnes were very close friends as girls in California."

"We were. She was my first friend. Later I worked for her father, William, when he was directing films."

"What did you do?" I asked.

"I was the script girl," she said.

Lucia Chase did finance a ballet company called American Ballet Theater, and Agnes choreographed many ballets for them. Anthony Tudor and Hugh Laing were brought over from England to be part of the company, Tudor as choreographer and Laing as principal dancer.

When I got the play from the typist I found so many mistakes that I had to have it retyped, and that took another week. Mary read it as soon as I took it to her, and liked it.

My brother refused to stay in college in Iowa and insisted on coming to New York to study. Joe had moved out of the Waverly Place apartment and so I wrote my parents to let my brother come on and room with me and that I would help him find a part-time job to take care of his living expenses while he studied acting. He arrived in New York just after Thanksgiving. I went to Pennsylvania Station to meet him; he was all excited about New York, and began talking as soon as he saw me, telling me how much he appreciated my encouraging our parents to let him come.

"Dad said you were going to take me to meet Madame Daykarhanova and ask about studying with her."

"Daykarhanova and Jilinsky have split. They now each have a school, so you're going to have to meet both of them and make a decision where you want to study."

"You tell me what to do."

"I can't. I really have to stay out of it. I owe them both a great deal."

He went to see Daykarhanova first and she was gracious and charming, as only she could be, and he was very impressed. Then he went to see Jilinsky and he was also charming and gracious, and he offered him a full scholarship, so Tom decided to study with him.

The Katherine Dunham concerts were a great success, and the performances were sold out. Two weeks after the concerts ended, Mary called me to say she was scheduling *Texas Town* to open late in April and we would begin rehearsals sometime in March.

Texas Town is set in a small-town drugstore in the late 1930s. These drugstores were often the center of the town's social life. They opened early in the morning, seven or seven thirty, and stayed open until eleven at night. Doctors had their offices over the drugstores. In between patients, the doctor would come downstairs to visit with the idlers that invariably sat in the chairs in front, or inside on the counter stools. The drugstore in my play was modeled on three I knew in Wharton, and the characters were composites of people I had so often observed growing up.

The play tells the story of two brothers, vastly different in temperament, who are in love with the same girl. One wants nothing more than to lead a conventional small-town life, the other feels suffocated by the town and its culture and wants badly to get away. The Depression is making all such hopes more difficult. The stories of the other characters, who come in and out of the drugstore, are explored as a kind of counterpart to the central story.

The play had twenty-two characters and we had to cast some parts outside the company. We had interviews and auditions and after a week completed our casting.

Harry Carey, Jr., was one of the actors we brought in from outside. He had been in "Railroads on Parade" with me and we became friends. His father, Harry Carey, Sr., was a famous cowboy star in early films and had come East to appear in the Theater Guild's revival of *Ah, Wilderness*. His wife, Olive, his daughter, and Harry Jr. had come with him.

Many of the actors, particularly the men, had to have part-time jobs. The company could pay no salaries at all.

I was cast as Ray Case, the boy that wanted to leave the town. I became so involved with working on my part I almost forgot I was the playwright.

The actors were fond of the play and there was a feeling of optimism in the company. A week before we were to leave Sixty-ninth Street for the Humphrey-Weidman Studio, Mary scheduled our first run-through and Harry Carey, Jr., asked if his mother could attend. "All right," Mary said. "As long as she understands it's our first run-through and it will be rough at times." Later Mary said she had consented as she knew Mrs. Carey was wealthy, and as we were still looking for money for the production, she thought if his mother liked it she might be willing to invest.

Mrs. Carey arrived with the actress-singer Lotte Lenya. They were both elegantly dressed. Mary made a speech before starting the rehearsal to say that this was a working run-through and the actors could stop if they wanted to. For some reason I began to panic; I was not so destructively frightened as I had been at the *Swing Your Lady* rehearsal, but I was unconcentrated, feeling very inadequate, and I thought I performed miserably.

I got through the run-through somehow and Mrs. Carey and Lotte Lenya left without saying good-bye or making any comment whatsoever.

The next morning Harry Carey, Jr., phoned me before rehearsals to say he was sorry, but his family was leaving suddenly for California as his father had a job in a film and he wanted Harry Jr. to go with them. We found another actor that same afternoon to replace him and rehearsals continued harmoniously.

The opening night of *Texas Town* was the first time we had performed the play before an audience. We knew from the responses to our mailings that we would have a full house. Florence Odets was working with our company now and she told us that her brother Clifford and Lee and Paula Strasberg would be there. We also knew that Brooks Atkinson, the critic for *The New York Times,* was coming.

Beulah Weil, who played my mother in the play and who always suffered severely from stage fright, said on her first entrance opening night she was in total terror and thought she might faint, but when she came onstage and saw the terror in my eyes, she roused herself some way and was able to continue. If I was in terror I wasn't aware of it, at least not after the first few moments onstage.

The friends that came back after the performance were friendly, some enthusiastic. Florence said her brother and the Strasbergs had been very impressed by the play and the performance. The edition of *The New York Times* that carried the reviews of plays didn't go on the stands in those days until three in the morning. After the opening I went with my brother and some of the other actors in the company to a bar to wait for Brooks Atkinson's review. At two thirty my brother went down to Times Square to get a copy of the paper. He was gone almost an hour, but when he returned we could see from the expression on his face he was bringing good news. He read the notice aloud to us, which said:

Even in real life virtue is occasionally rewarded and "Texas Town" is a case in point. As acted last evening in an informal theater at 108 West Sixteenth Street, it does considerable honor to a group of tenacious players dubbed the American Actors Company. For four years they have held together, industriously rehearsing in a loft over a garage. Three years ago this correspondent happened to see them in a dismal production of Edith Hamilton's version of "The Trojan Women." To put it mildly that episode was not encouraging.

But now they are acting a simply written narrative play by Horton Foote, who is one of their own actors, and it suits them admirably. In a general sort of way it is the drama of a young man who tries desperately to leave a small town in Texas and find some work—any work to do. But that is only the thread of a narrative that runs through an engrossing

portrait of small town life. It is set in a drugstore where old
and young people naturally congregate for gossip and relaxation. Although Mr. Foote has no particular ax to grind, his
play gives a real and languid impression of a town changing
in its relation to the world—the old stock drifting down
the economic and social scale, the young people at loose
ends in an organization that does not employ them.

If "Texas Town" does not derive from Mr. Foote's per-
sonal experiences and observations, he is remarkably inven-
tive. For none of the parts is stock theater, except perhaps
the part he plays himself without much talent and with no
originality. And it is impossible not to believe absolutely in
the reality of his characters. The melancholy doctor who
drinks in the back room, the hearty judge and his cronies,
the bored wife who is looking for excitement, the chatter-
ing girls, the bumptious boys, the sharp edges of bad feeling that cut through the neighborhood leisure, the quick
impulses of emotion, the sense of drifting without purpose
or direction—these are truths of small town life that Mr.
Foote has not invented.

Generally the good works of groups like the American
Actors Company appeal to a reviewer's good-will more than
to his happiness. But Mr. Foote's quiet play is an able evoca-
tion of a part of life in America, and most of the acting is
interesting and thoughtful. Will Hare's drugstore clerk,
Loraine Stuart's young business girl, Frederick Campbell's
judge, Dwight Marfield's ne'er-do-well, Roland Wood's
doctor, Patricia Coates' drifting young matron, Bettina
Prescott's coquette, Casey Walter's drugstore cowboy, John

Hampshire's dominie, Beulah Weil's possessive Mother are all well acted with insight into character and Randall Steplight's aging Negro is superb.

Character parts are the curse of young actors' groups. This performance is not free of them, and some of the best acting is occasionally over-accented with detail. But it is something to walk in out of Sixteenth Street in New York into the waiting and idle atmosphere of a small town in Texas. Mr. Foote and the American Actors Company have performed that feat of magic. If they do not feel encouraged, this department does.

I had mixed emotions about the review. I was delighted, of course, about his liking the play and his response to the direction of Mary and the other actors, but I was hurt by what he said about my acting. I pretended that it made no difference at all to me, but it did, of course. Mary and the others reassured me that I was doing some of my best work as an actor and that what he had to say was puzzling to them.

The next day I got a call from the Shubert Office requesting a copy of my play and later in the week, after they had read it, they took an option on it for Broadway. They let me know, however, they would require some changes, which they would discuss with me later.

Agnes de Mille rolled her eyes when I told her and warned me to beware. She had choreographed a musical for the Shuberts and had a very low opinion of them.

After *Texas Town* closed, *American Legend* moved into the Humphrey-Weidman Theater and began the final weeks of rehearsals. I attended all of them and was very impressed with what the company was doing. I thought the dances Agnes had choreographed were lovely and touching, and graced with that sly, slightly wicked humor that Agnes always seemed to achieve so effortlessly in her best work. The whole concept for the evening had been Mary's, and I was dazzled by the scope and vitality of what she had achieved. The music and its performers were always affecting and sometimes deeply moving.

I made friends with the dancers Jerry Robbins, Ray Harrison, Katherine Litz, and Sybil Shearer. I was in awe of their technical and performing skills. Jerry, Ray, and I continued our friendship long after *American Legend* and Agnes and I became lifelong friends, a friendship that lasted until her death. I visited with her often in the last years of her life in her apartment on East Ninth Street. Though crippled by a stroke, she continued working, writing, and choreographing.

The opening of *American Legend* was received with great enthusiasm by the audience. Atkinson was there again and wrote in his review:

> Having an idle Spring night on their hands, the young ladies and gentlemen of the American Actors Company staged what they dub "American Legend" in the studio playhouse at 108 West Sixteenth Street last evening. This is the group that has latterly been playing "Texas Town" to general satisfaction. Although "American Legend" sounds historical, it is really a bill of light entertainment—dance, song and drama, with notable assistance from Richard Hale and Agnes de Mille.
>
> Miss De Mille's excellent choreographic ideas are a great

help to "American Legend," especially when she is wearing country manners. This column is likely to feel uncomfortably stern before pieces of marine artifice like "Clipper Sailing," although Joseph Anthony dances a wonderful sailor; and it looks with some austerity upon nymphs and dryads, although Miss De Mille and Katherine Litz dance their aquatics with extraordinary skill. But what could be more enchanting than the country dance that opens the program and what could be more rousing than the spontaneous good-humored frontier dance at the conclusion? In a word, nothing.

Despite several gestures toward art that are a pain at least in the neck in "American Legend," there is enough fresh and joyous material in the bill to warrant an inquiring visit next Sunday afternoon or evening.

The Montowese Playhouse in Montowese, Connecticut, had been a prosperous summer theater for a number of years. It was run by the owners of a nearby hotel. They had not been happy with the management of the theater the last two summers and had heard of the American Actors Company. They had a director in place, but wanted us to manage the season and use our actors in the plays with an occasional guest star.

We had a meeting and decided it was a profitable thing to do since it would earn money for the company and give the actors summer salaries.

We opened the season with a revival of George Abbott's *Broadway,* and followed that with Joe Anthony and me doing *The Male Animal* by James Thurber. This was the last time we acted together. He left the next week for California and a movie job at Metro Goldwyn Mayer.

I was in eight plays that summer when the desire to act left me as suddenly as it had appeared all those years ago. I had become obsessed now with writing and had begun working on a new play for the company.

There were no off- or off-off-Broadway theaters in New York City then except for the American Actors Company and we became deluged with inquiries from actors and playwrights hoping to work with us.

In those days critics, it seemed, were always looking for the great American novel or the great American play. What would it be? When would it appear? Reviews often began with "so and so's play (or novel) showed great promises at the beginning and we thought here at last was the great American play (or novel), but alas, after the first act (or the first forty pages), we were sadly disappointed."

That had happened to Arnold Sundgaard when his play *Everywhere I Roam,* directed by Marc Connelly, was produced on Broadway. After the first act all the critics thought they had found the great American play, but by the end had lost their enthusiasm.

Arnold was interested in the work of our company and we became close friends. He had two daughters by a first marriage and was expecting another child by his present wife. He was struggling to make some kind of a living for his family, and I wondered if I could ever be as secure and optimistic as he seemed with so many responsibilities. He was thirty-two, amiable, and loved to talk. He had been writing for a number of years and had been awarded many fellowships. The Group Theater had shown interest in his plays and he had recently been commissioned by the Michael Chekhov Company to write a play for them. I wanted to spend all my time writing now and asked him about applying for a Guggenheim. He explained the application process and said I would have to summarize the story of the play I intended to write. He said that's why he never applied for a Guggenheim, because he thought summarizing a play before it was written would kill it for him. He had a new play, *The First Crocus,* that he wanted to give to our company, but it was under option for Broadway. "When it is done, Perry Wilson is to be in it," he said.

"She's long gone now," I said. "I don't think she'll ever come back to the company."

"She's still a member, isn't she?" he said.

"Yes, but she works all the time now on Broadway," I said.

"Get used to that," he said. "That happened to the Group. It's inevitable, the talented ones, or the more talented ones get offers and leave. It happened in the Moscow Art Theater. Look how many left Stanislavsky—Michael Chekhov, Boleslavsky, Meyerhold, your teachers."

"Jilinsky left for political reasons," I said.

"Whatever the reason, it is a fact of life they leave," he said.

"How long have you been writing plays?" I asked.

"Since college. I started then. From college I went to the Barter Theater in Virginia. I had some of my first productions there. *Everywhere I Roam* was first done there," he said.

"Did it upset you when it failed in New York?" I asked.

"No," he said.

"How come?"

"Because of what Marc Connelly wanted to do with the last half of the play. I knew then it would fail."

"What did he want to do?"

"Change everything that had worked at Barter."

"Why?"

"Because he thought he could make it commercial this way. Make money."

I had begun my meetings with the representative for the Shuberts over changes for *Texas Town*. I was not happy with the suggestions. I went to Arnold to see what he thought.

"Arnold, I need some more advice," I asked him one day.

"Yes."

"I don't like the changes that the Shuberts are asking for *Texas Town*."

"Then don't do them," he said. "I wish I had said no to Connelly, but I needed the money. That's always the problem, you need the money. Do you need money?"

"Yes, I do."

"Well, tighten your belt and move on. You're still a bachelor. Wait until you have a wife and children, then it gets harder."

I don't remember when I first met Tennessee Williams, or how he heard about the American Actors Company. I know that for a time he was interested in Mary directing his play *You Touched Me*. I had read some of his one-act plays and I was particularly fond of *This Property Is Condemned.* I knew, too, about the Theater Guild's production of his *Battle of Angels,* and the horror stories that happened during its tryout in Boston. He once described the chaos of the opening night of his play there, with that peculiar, particular laugh of his punctuating each tale of disaster. He was as poor now as Arnold or I but he reacted to it quite differently, laughing his way through all of his complaints of poverty.

There was about Arnold still something of the midwestern farm boy, while Tennessee was to me a complete original, something I had never seen before. He knew of Ramon Naya's plays and thought he was a genius. I heard of the poet Hart Crane from him for the first time, and I never heard him speak of another writer with such feeling, not even Chekhov. He seemed devoted to Mary Hunter and the American Actors Company, and came around whenever he was in New York. He was Arnold's age and had been writing plays as long, or longer, and I think he had already received an award from the Group Theater for his one-act plays. He was kind and generous to me, sharing his knowledge and his experience as willingly as Arnold did. Later when I was working on *Marcus Strachen,* a most complicated play, which I was never able to finish to my satisfaction, he took a great interest in the play and its progress.

In late fall of 1941 I finished *Out of My House.* It was in four parts. I showed it to Mary and she felt the company should make it their next production. It required a cast of eighteen and four different sets. Joe Anthony was back from Hollywood and had not had a happy time. He was given the play to read and he agreed to design the sets. To open the play in January, which was Mary's wish, meant we had to be in rehearsal by mid-December. Actors were cast and instead of one overall director, we decided (at least Mary did) that there should be three directors. She wanted to direct the last play, and suggested that Jane Rose direct the second and that I should direct the first and the third. We met at Mary's on December seventh to discuss final casting and rehearsal schedules, when someone called Mary and told her to turn on the radio. She did and we heard that the Japanese had bombed Pearl Harbor. The play was forgotten and we sat waiting for word from the president. We all felt certain that we would be in the war, that it was only a matter of hours. Would there be a production of my play now? Should there be? Mary, always level-headed, calmed us down. She said if war was declared it would be months before a draft could be functioning and she felt we should go ahead with our plans to produce the play. And that's what we did. We went into rehearsal as scheduled at the Humphrey-Weidman Studio and Joe Anthony designed the sets and began building them.

Atkinson came again to the opening and said in his review:

In case any one asks Horton Foote, "How's your last act?" he can reply, "Stunning." Mr. Foote is the young man who disturbed the calm of last Spring with an interesting play titled "Texas Town." Since then he has been in Texas long enough to gather the material for a sort of successor, "Out of My House," which the American Actors Company put on last evening at the Studio, 108 West Sixteenth Street. The new play, written in four parts, is loosely-contrived, and sometimes seems to be a footless variety show. But after he has portrayed the decadence of "certain levels," as the program calls them, of a Southern cotton town, Mr. Foote pulls himself together in a vibrant and glowing last act that is compact and bitterly realistic and also remarkably well played. Although "Texas Town" was a better play than "Out of My House," none of "Texas Town" was so good as this last act.

The American Actors Company rented the first floor of a brownstone on Fifty-second Street, used the living room as an office, and rented out the bedrooms to members of the company. I shared one of the rooms with my brother. He was still studying with Jilinsky and had just finished playing in Lynn Riggs's *The Big Lake* at Jilinsky's Studio Theater, and had been offered a studio contract by Warner Brothers. As I remember the contract was for six months at fifty dollars a week, which sounded like a fortune to both of us. The day before he was to sign he got a notice from his draft board to appear for his physical. He passed the physical and a month later left for a training camp. Soon after, Joe Anthony and I received our draft notices.

I fully expected to be drafted, and I spent three weeks disposing of what little I owned. I turned over the drafts of a play I was working on to a friend that I knew would take care of them. My mother wrote me a positive letter, saying she was sure all would be well for both her sons.

Joe Anthony and I went for our physical together, but inside the induction center we were separated. I don't remember how long my physical took, but when at last it was over I reported to an officer. I stood waiting for the final acceptance, when he stamped on my record *rejected*. It was discovered I had a hernia, which I knew nothing about. I was given my clothes to put back on and was told I could go home. I was in a daze. For a month I had prepared myself for the army, had gotten letters from my brother and other friends saying the army wasn't half bad, and I was looking forward to it. I dressed and on my way out I saw Joe Anthony in the distance marching away. He had been accepted.

I called Mary Hunter right away and went to her apartment. I told her I felt lost and totally disoriented. She said she understood, but counseled me to get back to writing as soon as possible. She loaned me some money to tide me over until I could find work. I got a job running an elevator in a Park Avenue apartment building. I started work at six in the evening and worked until six in the morning. All the tenants were usually in for the night by twelve, so from twelve to six I wrote without interruption.

The other men who worked in the apartment were much older and were curious about what I was doing. And the tenants became aware also and asked me many questions. One of the tenants was Oscar Serlin, whose production of *Life With Father* was still running at the Empire Theater, and at least once a week he inquired about the progress of the play and made me promise that when it was finished I would let him read it. When I finished, Mary read the play and said, "We'll do it right away."

I called the play *Mamie Borden,* and it only had six characters, which was a relief to Mary. She cast it with Hilda Vaughn, Jeanne Tufts, Freeman Hammond, Constance Dowling, Jacqueline Andre, and Richard Hart. Jeanne Tufts was the only member of our company, the rest were unknown to me. Hilda objected to the play being called *Mamie Borden.* She was afraid people would think it would be about Lizzie Borden and her ax and wanted to call the play *Only the Heart.* Mary agreed with her and I reluctantly gave in. The Humphrey-Weidman Studio was not available, so we rented the Provincetown Playhouse.

We opened December fifth on schedule and this time all the major New York critics were there. Lewis Nichols, who had taken Atkinson's place at the *Times,* was generally friendly, but reserved. The other reviews were very positive and because of the reviews we had many inquiries from uptown producers.

Helen Thompson, who had earlier been with the Group Theater, had joined us now as a producer of *Only the Heart,* and she hoped to move it uptown to Broadway.

The third day of our run she called me in great excitement to say that the producer Luther Green had seen the play and was very taken with it and if he could get Pauline Lord to play the lead he would bring it to Broadway. I had mentally made a decision not to go with any producer that would not keep Mary as director.

"What about Mary directing?" I asked.

"He didn't mention that," she said. "We can discuss that after Miss Lord has seen the play."

"Is she going to see the play?" I asked.

"Yes. He's bringing her tonight," Helen said.

I had been almost obsessed with Pauline Lord ever since I had seen her in *Ethan Frome.* Daykarhanova and Soloviova often spoke of her acting in class and said that Stanislavsky felt that Pauline Lord and Laurette Taylor were the two American actresses that understood instinctively his system, and Stark Young in writing about the Moscow Art Theater felt that the realistic acting of Joseph Jefferson, Pauline Lord, David Warfield, and Laurette Taylor was as fine as any of the Russians. In the spring of 1940 she had opened in *Suspect* in New York, and though the reviews were not good I couldn't wait to see it. The play was set in a remote country house, and she played a recluse whose privacy is suddenly invaded by a reporter, intent on interviewing her. In the past she had been charged with murder, killing her victim with an ax à la Lizzie Borden. She had been acquitted, many years have passed, and now she seems demure and frail and anything but a murderer. The play consists of the reporter trying to establish once and for all if she is the murderer, but finally gets nowhere and leaves. Up until then I found nothing very impressive, certainly not the play, and Miss Lord seemed passive, as if defeated by the material, almost as if she were saying to herself, How can I connect with this character and this silly play I've been given to work with? When the reporter left, though, and she went out into the yard to the wood pile, she seized an ax, and began chopping the wood with such violence and fury that you know she was the murderer. Those moments made up for all the dreariness of what had gone before.

She came to the play with Luther Green and sent word she would like to see me at two the next day at her hotel in the East Forties. I hadn't slept much the night before the meeting and arrived at the hotel a half hour before two. I walked around the block a number of times, and at two I went in to the hotel desk.

"I'm here to see Miss Lord," I said.

"Who?" the man behind the desk asked.

"Miss Pauline Lord," I said.

"What's your name?" he asked.

"Horton Foote," I said.

He rang her room, and I heard him say I was in the lobby. He turned to me then and said, "She's expecting you" and gave me the room number. I thanked him and got into the elevator and gave the operator the floor number. I got off the elevator at her floor and started down the corridor toward her room. I had been practicing all morning just what I would say to her when we met, but suddenly I couldn't remember any of the speeches I had prepared. I was in a panic and almost went back down to the lobby. The palms of my hands were perspiring, and I turned around to leave when I said to myself, Wipe the palms of your hands and pull yourself together. You don't have to impress her with your words. She's seen the play. She either likes it or she doesn't. I paused then and wiped my palms on my pants and continued on until I came to her door. I rang the bell, my heart beating, my throat dry, wondering if I could speak without stuttering. Miss Lord was dressed simply, and she seemed glad to see me and suddenly my fear left me. She said, "Come in, Mr. Foote, you are very talented," and I thought of all things, Is this frail, demure woman, the same one that seized the ax with such strength and fury in *Suspect?* I smiled and thanked her. I came into the room then and she pointed to a sofa and asked me to have a seat and I sat down and she sat on the sofa, too, and I told her I had seen her in *Ethan Frome* and I thought it was the most moving performance I had ever seen. She thanked me and smiled, and said she was glad I had liked her performance, that she had difficulty finding plays that she felt were right for her. She said good plays are rare, and good plays that she felt right for her even rarer.

She said she'd had a restless, miserable night thinking over my play, which Luther Green thought was very right for her, and she wanted to agree as she liked the play very much, but in all conscience couldn't, and she hoped I would understand that.

I wanted to find the words and the wisdom to convince her she was wrong, but in truth listening to her speak, with such clarity and humility, and such sure knowledge of what was right for her and what wasn't, I knew, as much as it disappointed me to admit it, she was surely right.

I thought of our meeting that day once again when I saw her at the National Theater in Washington, D.C., as Amanda in *The Glass Menagerie,* a part she was certainly very right for.

I was living and working in Washington in a small theater I had helped start. When *The Glass Menagerie* arrived at the National Theater, I was so busy with chores in my theater that I didn't plan to go see the play. Laurette Taylor had by then been so identified with Amanda, that I thought any other actress in the part, even Pauline Lord, couldn't be as interesting. However, John Hampshire, a friend of mine, was stage manager and he called me and said, "You'd better come and see this. This is a kind of phenomenon. As different as Miss Taylor as can be but just as brilliant."

And so I went and from the very moment Miss Lord entered the stage saying lines I knew so well: "Tom, we can't say grace until you come to the table," I knew I was in for something very special. Every moment was illuminated with what she alone could bring to a part. She was no better than Miss Taylor, perhaps, but more fragile and more vulnerable and, to me, more tragic in her desperation. Then, too, there were moments of great tenderness and beauty. I went to see it three times.

John Hampshire was also admiring of her work, and was devoted to her. He said the last time she had toured had been with the Theater Guild's production of *Strange Interlude.* The road was very prosperous then and she had been given her own coach. Now in wartime all she had was a pullman in crowded trains and no one to meet her at the stations. He said he always managed to be with her and help her with her luggage. He said no one in the New York management had been near her in spite of her enthusiastic reception on the road. I asked if Tennessee had seen her performances and he said no. I wrote Tennessee that night and said he should come to Washington to see her, but he never replied. John insisted that I meet her. I went backstage with him after seeing the third performance. I didn't remind her of our meeting long ago, but did tell her over and over again how extraordinary I thought her performance was, and what her acting meant to me. She seemed pleased, and smiled that sad smile of hers. Then I said, "You must take this play into New York. New York should see you in this play." (I knew from John producers had been talking to her about doing so.)

"No," she said in that quiet plaintive way she had of talking. "It was bad enough when she was alive, but now she's dead they've made a perfect martyr of her."

She was speaking of Laurette Taylor, of course, who had recently died. Miss Lord, too, was dead a few years after. She was sixty years old.

CHAPTER 12

Valerie Bettis   Martha Graham

During rehearsals of *American Legend,* I would often go out into the foyer of the theater where Doris Humphrey was usually at work writing letters or going over class schedules. I had heard Mary say that she and her partner, Charles Weidman, had been trained by Ruth St. Denis and was a member of her company at the same time as Martha Graham. I knew, too, that Doris Humphrey and Martha Graham were considered the two great choreographers of that time, and that they were rivals. Each had a loyal almost fanatical following. I had seen Martha Graham dance several times, but I had never seen Doris Humphrey or Charles Weidman. Although both Graham and Humphrey had been trained by Ruth St. Denis, their evolving techniques were by now radically and aggressively different. Dancers and non-dancers argued about the merits of the two.

In the two years we were in and out of the Humphrey-Weidman Studio, I found myself more and more seeking Doris out and asking her questions about dance and choreography. I went to her concerts whenever they were given.

Nona Sherman, a member of the Humphrey-Weidman Company, was preparing a concert of her own at the YMHA, where so many young dancers in those days made their concert debuts. One of her solos was based on a poem by Carl Sandburg, *The People, Yes.* She knew that I had been an actor and asked if I would read the poem as she danced. I agreed and we rehearsed several times and then on a Sunday afternoon we performed the piece at the YMHA. In the audience that afternoon was Pearl Primus, a young black dancer, who was getting a great deal of attention. She came backstage after the performance and asked if I would read the poem *Strange Fruit* to a dance she was choreographing and I agreed. The afternoon Pearl Primus gave her concert at the YMHA, Valerie Bettis was in the audience with the pianist-composer Bernardo Segall. They came backstage afterward and were very complimentary and asked if I would be willing to work with her. I said yes, and this began one of the most meaningful associations of my life. She had been trained by another of the great modern dance teacher-choreographers, Hanya Holm. Hanya was German, a student of Mary Wigman, of whom Charlotte Sturges had been so fond. Hanya had been in New York City for many years and had her own company. She didn't approve of either the Humphrey or Graham techniques. Valerie was devoted to Hanya, but also a great admirer of Graham. She was not as enthusiastic about Humphrey.

I met Valerie at her studio and she gave me the poem *The Des-*

perate Heart by John Malcolm Brinnin, which I was to read as she danced. Bernardo Segall had written a very moving score, which he played for me. We spent the whole afternoon working on the timing of words and music with the dance.

We performed *The Desperate Heart* first at the Humphrey-Weidman Studio, in a concert sponsored by *The Dance Observer,* Louis Horst's magazine. On the program were three other young dancers: Erick Hawkins, Pearl Lang, and Virginia Johnson. The theater was packed. *The Dance Observer* critic had this to say about Valerie:

> In presenting another quartette of young dancers at the Studio Theater March 24, 25 and 26, *The Dance Observer* unwrapped a prize package of the year, a solo by Valerie Bettis entitled "The Desperate Heart." On a bare and darkened stage, a wounded, famished soul dances its anguish, its rage, its despair in recitative to words of bitter confession from the wings. The movement spreads as the piano takes up the cry. Fragments of the words return and the solo is over, an explosion of dance fire that sent the audience into cheers.

That night after the performance we went to dinner and Valerie told me of her desire to create a series of theater pieces, works that combined words, music, and dance. She asked if I had anything that she might use. I had recently written a one-act play called *Daisy Lee,* and I brought it to her the next day. She read it right away and said she wanted to do it. Working with her on the play, using music and dance to enhance the play as she did, made a great impression on me. I began to work on a full-length play for her using the same techniques.

Tennessee Williams came in and out of New York now with some regularity and I was making no money working with dancers and Tennessee, who also needed to make money, suggested we both might get jobs working together on a farm for the summer. "That," he said, "would give us some money and would help the war effort." He had worked once on a chicken ranch and although that hadn't turned out well, the idea of farm work of another kind appealed to him. He left town again for St. Louis and I agreed to see about farm employment.

That spring the American Actors Company was approached by Sanford Meisner about coproducing Ben Simkhovitch's play *The Playboy of Newark,* with Meisner directing and Russell Collins starring. Simkhovitch had raised money for the production. None of us in the company were very enthusiastic about the play, but all of us were anxious to work with Meisner and Russell Collins. The company asked me to serve as producer.

I knew that Sanford Meisner and Russell Collins had both been distinguished members of the Group Theater. Sanford, or Sandy, as everyone called him, was a fine actor that I had seen in two of the Odets plays done by the Group. He was now teaching acting at the Neighborhood Playhouse. Russell Collins I had seen in *The Star-Wagon,* with Lillian Gish and Burgess Meredith at the Empire Theater.

From the beginning, Russell argued with Sandy about his direction and how the part was to be played. Sandy got up one day to illustrate for Russell a piece of business he wanted him to do, and Russell refused, saying, "That's how you'd play the part, not how I'd play it. If that's what you want, then you play the part yourself." It was not a very happy company. The reviews were not good and we closed soon after opening.

I became very fond of Sandy and after rehearsals I'd often ask him questions about directing and acting and the Group Theater. He asked if I had a one-act play that he might direct with his students. I gave him *Miss Lou,* which he liked and had his students perform at the playhouse.

When Sandy got acting jobs he would take a leave from his teaching at the playhouse. In his absence, he asked me to direct his advanced students in plays.

Mrs. Rita Morgenthau was dean of the Playhouse School, and at the end of each school year she always commissioned a playwright to write a play incorporating all the disciplines of the school: music, dance, and acting. She asked me to write and direct a play for the coming spring, for which Louis Horst would compose a score and Martha Graham would choreograph. The play I wrote was called *The Lonely,* and it was, I thought, quite radical in its form. She seemed pleased with it and gave it to Martha Graham to read. She called to say that Martha was pleased, too, and it had been given to Louis Horst to compose a score.

I didn't meet Martha Graham until the play's first rehearsal. She was forty-seven at the time, old for a dancer, but her greatest works and performances were still ahead. An austere beauty, always smartly dressed, smaller than I had imagined, with raven black hair. She was very gracious about my play and said she thought I would be pleased with Louis Horst's score.

* * *

I asked the actors at the first rehearsal to read the play through for us. Martha sat beside me listening, and when it was finished, suggested I spend the next few days staging the play and when that was done she would come again and we'd begin our work together. When she returned she watched a run-through and then began to work with the actors transforming my play, saying at one point, "Don't let me do too much; I have a tendency to overdo." I was spellbound. She took those students and my play and through her genius turned it into something unique and very beautiful. When Louis Horst arrived with the score, we showed him the play and he was equally impressed. His score was haunting and powerful and just right for the play.

Martha and I both lived in the Village, and often after rehearsals we'd take the Fifth Avenue bus downtown together. I asked her a great many questions about theater and dance during those bus rides, and she was always generous in sharing her knowledge.

Louis Horst and I became close friends. He was older than Martha, gray-haired, stout, and seemed gruff when you first knew him. He composed many of her early dance scores, and was devoted to her and her choreography and to the whole of the modern dance movement. He lived in Greenwich Village, too, on Twelfth Street, as I remember, and had a dachshund that went with him on his walks about the Village. He was devoted also to Valerie Bettis and a great champion of her work. He was the editor of *The Dance Observer* and, knowing my growing interest in dance, asked me to write for it.

Martha Graham, Louis Horst, Doris Humphrey, Charles Weidman, Hanya Holm, all the great modern dance choreographers and performers of that period, lived mostly on what they earned from teaching. Their recitals, too, had to be financed by their teaching and occasional foundation grants. There was never enough money, it seemed. Graham and Humphrey often had to sew their own costumes.

We'd had no success in interesting producers to take *Only the Heart* to Broadway without a star. In the meantime, Constance Dowling had gone to Los Angeles, Richard Hart was cast in *Dark of the Moon* for Broadway, and Hilda Vaughn had signed for a play Elia Kazan was directing.

In the late winter I received a letter from Jacques Therie, who said he had read my play and wanted to meet. I called him and we made a date the next day for lunch.

Jacques Therie, in his late fifties, was from Paris and said he was known there as the George Kaufman of France because of his success at working on plays there and making them hits. At lunch he told me he admired my play very much, and felt with a little work I would have a great Broadway success. He said he had been asked by Charles Boyer to work on a film they had at one time talked about in Paris, and he proposed that I come with him to Hollywood and live at his house while we worked on my play. He then met with Mary and charmed her and she advised me to go.

The day I agreed to go to California, I received this letter from Tennessee Williams:

April 5, 1943

Tovarich—
How are you going on our Back-to-the-Farm movement? I am relying on you to get the ball rolling as the more I think

of a bucolic summer the more it intrigues me. Let us if possible find one in the vicinity of a summer play-house and a beach and let us determine to work on one big problem (that is, one each) and not a lot of little pieces so that when the summer is over we shall have something significant completed. When I was working on the play in Macon last summer, I started out with a day-by-day schedule which I tacked on the wall over my desk and would not get up from the typewriter each day till I had checked off the scene assigned. I think this discipline actually works, when you have a free season. It would be an interesting experiment for each to supervise the other's revisions. I think good professional criticism is half the battle—and I have never really had it.

I am taking it easy here, not writing at all since I got here. Reading a lot of Lawrence, his letters and novels, and absorbing my Grandparents' reminiscences. I have no friends here, see nobody, but every afternoon about five thirty or six I go down on the river-front and have a beer and listen to a juke-box in one of the dusky old bars that face the railroad tracks and the levee. That is the only part of St. Louis which has any charm. I feel much calmer. I want to continue this sort of life—quiet and contemplative, I mean—for about five months. By that time I should know what I want to do with my life from now on and have the resolution to do it.

Drifting is no good!

Write me—

Always,
Tenn.

I had forgotten all about our working on a farm, and was about to write that I was going to California, when I got a second letter:

April 24, 1943

Dear Horton:

Is the island of Manhattan trembling with the rage of Mr. Gering? I feel as though it were. I suspect it is even registered on the seismograph in St. Louis. I was supposed to be back in New York two weeks ago and the date of my departure is still not definitely set, though I must certainly leave before May 2nd when my Father returns from the West Coast.

I am very excited by the news of the company plans. They sound excellent to me and you may certainly count on any support I can give. My only question is concerning the change of name. Since the American Actors Company has received so much honor under its present title, I wonder why you want to change it. It seems to me that the word "Playwrights" is too exclusive in an organization that also contains characters like Mary Hunter and Helen Thompson and Jane Rose. The emphasis should be on a brilliant concert of direction, management, acting, and playwrighting. I wish you could think of a title that would mean "Art Theater," as distinguished from commercial, without exactly saying "Art Theater." The most palpable and discouraging fact in the New York theater is that no art theater is in existence at the present time. You promise to establish one and you have already taken notable steps in that direction— Why not let the emphasis be modestly but plainly focused on that object and accomplishment?

I have been working with tigerish fury on "The Gentleman Caller," it has become a fully-developed play almost of usual length. It has at least one part in it for you and maybe two, if you can imagine such a thing.

Did I tell you the pay-off with Gering? I had told him I would have to drop the war play. Then I discovered I hadn't money enough to get home on, so I had to tell him I had changed my mind and get another fifteen dollars out of him. Now I must pay back the fifteen or go on with the wretched business. When I think of it I could blow my brains out!

Listen, if you can get a farm-job that is only for you, for God's sake, take it! I mean don't make my employment conditional, because it may easily be impossible to find anybody who would want both of us. That would be wonderful, but you mustn't pass up a good chance holding out for it.

I have to be very careful this summer, live as quietly and healthfully as possible, as I am terribly tired and run down and can't get rid of my cough. If I don't take it fairly easy, I will be doing "Camille" next season at the Provincetown. Wouldn't that be something!

Are you going to let me see "Michael Strahan" when I return? I am very anxious to see what you have done with it. I have great faith in the ultimate script and think you should devote the summer to it if it isn't right yet.

How about contacting Naya for a script? Disagreeable as he is, he is like a box of roses in the luminous dark and ought to be reclaimed from that munitions plant. I cannot believe that he is through with the theater. At any rate, I don't think the theater is through with him. There is a primitive power in his writing that immediate criticism cannot destroy. He may be the Rimbaud of American drama.

We must remember that a new theater is coming after the war with a completely new criticism, thank God. The singular figures always stand a good chance when there are sweeping changes.

Keep your ear to the ground and concentrate on honesty till you know what else is coming!

All these people are going, going,—GONE!

Maybe we are too, but—

En Avant!

I wrote him at once that I would probably be in Los Angeles for the summer working on *Only the Heart,* and heard back from him that his agent had gotten him a six-month contract with Metro Goldwyn Mayer and he would see me on the coast.

Jacques Therie had a house in Los Angeles in Laurel Canyon, with a guesthouse where I was to stay. We had discussed my play on the train, and the changes he suggested seemed to me to not improve the play at all.

He wanted Dorothy Gish for the lead and promised, if I would make the changes, he would see that she read it. I was left alone to work on the play as he was busy with Boyer at the studio.

Tennessee Williams had started work at Metro Goldywn Mayer and was given impossible assignments. Neither of us had cars but we managed somehow to see each other. He took me to a party in Hollywood one night, and I met Margo Jones. Margo, with her enormous eyes and fast-talking vitality, overwhelmed me on our first meeting. She was devoted to Tennessee and was full of plans for a theater of her own where she promised to do wonderful work and produce all of our plays.

I was on salary in California and I saved every penny I could for when I got back to New York. Jacques was satisfied finally with my revisions and asked Dorothy Gish and Louis Calhern, who she was living with at the Garden of Allah, for tea. It was my first meeting with one of the Gish sisters and I was charmed, as I continued to be through the years, with both Lillian and Dorothy. Dorothy left with the play and promised to read it right away, which she did, and called to say it wasn't something she wanted to do. Jacques lost interest in the play and I went back to New York City. Mary read the play and thought it was improved. Helen Thompson read it and suggested Stella Adler for the lead. I had seen Miss Adler in the Group production of *Paradise Lost,* and I thought she was an interesting choice. She was sent the play and asked to see me. Helen felt it was a good sign. I went to Stella's apartment in midtown. She greeted me, dressed very glamorously, took my hand, and said, "Do I look like a bitter, frustrated woman?" I had to admit she didn't at all. She invited me into the apartment and I, like so many before me, fell completely under her spell. We talked about my play, which she liked, but felt wasn't right for her, and about the current theater, the demise of the Group, and the present state of acting. I left exhilarated. She was a brilliant talker and oh, oh, so bright. We remained friends.

Helen had found investors for the play. One of them was Dorothy Willard, who had been a backer for the Group. We were talking now about thousands of dollars, eighteen thousand, as I remember, for a play that had been produced earlier at the Provincetown for less than three thousand. Of course, now eighteen thousand wouldn't get you across the street in the New York theater—on Broadway or off—but this seemed astronomical at the time.

The search for a star continued and I went to Lake Ronkonkoma, Long Island, to be near Arnold Sundgaard, his wife, and new baby. I rented a room in a boardinghouse and spent my days working on a new play and in the evenings visiting with the Sundgaards.

When I went back to New York City in early winter I took a room at the Albert Hotel in the Village near Valerie Bettis and Bernardo Segall. They were married then and I was working on a play I called *In My Beginning,* which Valerie wanted to do. I spent almost every evening with them, talking about theater and dance on and on until late at night.

I met many interesting people at their apartment. John Cage, Merce Cunningham, Alma Mahler, who was Gustav Mahler's widow, Hanya Holm, Louis Horst, Nina Fanaroff, Bobby Lewis, Harry Holzman, who was executor of the abstract artist Piet Mondrian's estate, and who shocked me by saying he didn't care for Martha Graham's dancing or choreography, and much preferred Fred Astaire who was doing, what Holzman said, pure dance, joyful as all art should be. All of them were contemptuous of Broadway and the realistic theater, and thought it moribund and finished. I joined in on the attacks, wrote articles for *The Dance Observer,* denouncing current theater, and vowed to myself never to write another realistic play.

* * *

Only the Heart was finally financed and cast. June Walker, who had starred in *The Farmer Takes a Wife* with Henry Fonda and *Green Grow the Lilacs* with Franchot Tone and was cast as Mamie Borden, and Mildred Dunnock (who had been one of the original members of our company but had left after *Trojan Women*) joined us. Will Hare, from our company, was given Richard Hart's part. The actor cast as Mr. Borden had a heart attack in the middle of rehearsal and had to withdraw, and Maurice Wells, an assistant long ago to Gilmor Brown, replaced him.

A week later I got the news that my brother Tom Brooks was missing in action from a flight over Germany. I got in touch right away with my mother and father by phone and I offered to come home, but they insisted I stay on with the play, assuring me they were more than hopeful he was all right. They reminded me of two boys from our town who had been taken prisoner and that it had been several months before there had been any news of them. Weeks went by, then months and still no word. Several months after the war in Europe was over I had a call from a man who said he had been the pilot of the plane my brother was on as radio operator. He said that their plane was shot down over Germany. He was unharmed, but as he left the plane he saw my brother slumped over his instruments and he could see he was bleeding. He knew he had been wounded but couldn't say he was dead. He felt there was a slight chance my brother had been taken prisoner by the Germans, as he had been. I called my parents and told them all of this. My father wrote me that he feared my brother was dead, but my mother still hoped he was a prisoner somewhere. A month after the war in Japan was over that hope was ended. My brother's body had been found buried in Germany.

*   *   *

Arthur Hopkins came to a preview of *Only the Heart* and was very encouraging. I admired him so much that, though I had been insecure about the changes I had made and some of the new casting, I began to think I was wrong about my reservations.

Wrong or not, the reaction from the critics couldn't have been more disastrous. I took Valerie Bettis to the opening and we went to a diner in the Village after we'd seen the reviews and she was as severe as the critics. She didn't like the production at all and felt I was wasting my talent on this kind of play. I felt bruised and beaten. I was more and more interested now in another kind of theater and play, but I was still loyal to *Only the Heart* and to Mary and the company. Dorothy Willard put more money into the production to keep the play going, hoping we could find an audience. I agreed to waive any royalties and the actors took cuts in their salaries. The play ran for six weeks and then closed.

I had to find a job and knew that Sherwood Anderson and William Faulkner had worked in bookstores to support themselves while writing so I applied to the Doubleday chain. They made me night manager of their Pennsylvania Station store. A month later one of the clerks quit and late that afternoon a young woman, nineteen, wearing a gray Mexican peasant blouse and a blue striped peasant skirt, very tanned, her hair bleached from the sun, was sent over by the management as a possible replacement. She was a student at Radcliffe and had taken the semester off to come and work in New York. Her name was Lillian Vallish. I hired her on the spot and she went to work that night. After work (this was now midsummer), I asked if she would like to go for a walk by the river, but she declined. I asked her the next night and she accepted. Six weeks later I asked her to marry me, and she agreed, but wanted to postpone our marriage until she graduated from college in the fall. Her parents didn't approve of my profession or my prospects for making a proper living and wouldn't consent to our marriage and so, like my mother and father all those years before, we had to elope.

Tennessee Williams's contract at Metro Goldwyn Mayer was not renewed and he came back to New York with the finished *The Gentleman Caller,* which he was now calling *The Glass Menagerie.* He came by to see me at the bookstore, saying he had finished another uncommercial play. I asked to read it, and he brought me a copy. I read it and was very taken with it.

"Meisner is off doing another play," I told him. "I've been asked to direct his advanced class in a play and I'd like to do part of your play. I won't be able to cast the mother, but I can do the whole of *The Gentleman Caller* sequence, which is almost a one-act play."

"All right," he said.

I cast the scene with the student actors as scheduled. I had a few friends in to see a rehearsal and they were impressed. One of them met Tennessee later at the Provincetown Playhouse and told him he had seen the run-through and how much he liked the play and the actors. He said Tennessee was horrified, and said he had forgotten he had given me permission to do the play, that Audrey had just sold it that day to Eddie Dowling and she would be furious with him. I thought for sure he would tell me I would have to cancel my production, but he talked it over with Audrey and she decided it would be all right for me to go ahead, so two months before the Chicago premiere of *The Glass Menagerie,* I did the last half of the play at the Neighborhood Playhouse. Tony Randall saw it then, and whenever we meet, even to this day, he mentions having seen my production.

The afternoon of the play's New York opening, Tennessee came into the bookstore to say hello. I congratulated him on his Chicago success. He asked me if I would like to go to the opening, and I said I would. He asked me to meet him outside the lobby of the Playhouse Theater fifteen minutes before curtain. I got there promptly and I saw Tennessee standing alone on the street outside the lobby.

"Tennessee," I called.

He looked up and saw me. "Come on with me," he said.

He started down the alley of the Playhouse Theater, which leads to the stage door. I hurried to catch up with him and could see Eddie Dowling standing near the stage door, smoking a cigarette.

Tennessee called out to him, "Eddie."

"Yes, laddie," Dowling said.

"Do you know Horton Foote?" he asked.

"Oh, hello, laddie," Dowling said, looking at me and smiling as I was thinking all the while, What in God's name is Tennessee up to? when he asked, "Eddie, can you get him a seat for tonight?"

Now mind you, Eddie Dowling was one of the stars of the show, the codirector and coproducer, and the curtain was in fifteen minutes. I thought surely he would order us both out of the alley, but he didn't.

"Laddie," he said, "it's all sold out. Not a seat to be had." And then he turned to me, "Laddie," he said, "would you mind standing?"

"No, sir," I said.

He put out his cigarette and went inside the theater and in a few minutes came back and said, "I've arranged it. Tennessee, tell them at the front to let him in. He's to stand."

"Thank you, sir," I said, "and good luck tonight."

"Thank you, laddie," he said and went back into the theater.

"Let's hurry," Tennessee said as we went back down the alley to the theater.

Tennessee spoke to an usher and I was admitted and I saw the opening night of *The Glass Menagerie* standing at the back of the orchestra.

I met Margo Jones during the intermission and she invited me to her room at the Royalton Hotel after the opening. She said Tennessee and a few other friends would be there.

At the end of the play there was an ovation for the actors, the directors (Margo Jones and Eddie Dowling were listed as codirectors), and Tennessee.

I saw him briefly as he left the theater and told him I would see him later at Margo's. I'm not sure he heard me or what I had to say about his lovely play or Laurette Taylor's extraordinary performance. There were many people trying to get his attention and pay their respects.

When I got to Margo's room at the hotel she was already there with her friend Joanna Albus, and several other Texas friends. She was, of course, ecstatic at the reception of the play and the production. She said over and over the whole evening, while we waited for the arrival of Tennessee, "It's just the beginning, baby, of the great things we're going to all do together. I'm going to have a theater to do your plays and all the plays of the playwrights I believe in." Finally at two o'clock I decided Tennessee wasn't coming, although Margo kept insisting he would, and I left.

It was six years before I saw Tennessee again. I had moved to Washington and started a theater, and now married and with a family I was back in New York. I had been invited by my friend the composer Jerome Moross to an audition for backers of his musical *Gentlemen Be Seated.* Tennessee was there and he greeted me warmly and said I was one of the few people he knew that New York seemed to agree with. As we left the audition we promised to keep in touch with each other, but we didn't.

I wasn't to see him again until the opening night of *The Trip to Bountiful* at the Henry Miller Theater. We met in the lobby during the second-act intermission. He said he thought this was the best play I had written, and again we promised to keep in touch, but we didn't.

CHAPTER 13

Lillian Vallish Foote

My wife, Lillian Vallish, was born July 18, 1924, in Mount Carmel, Pennsylvania. She was the youngest child of Barbara and Walter Vallish. Her father, born in Poland, had come to the United States as a very young man. He had graduated from college in Poland, but the only work he could find in America was in the Pennsylvania coal mines. His marriage to his wife, Barbara, had been arranged by her parents. She had little schooling, but was bright and ambitious. They had seven children. Two boys died in infancy, the remaining five were girls: Barbara, Polly, Dorothy, Rita, and Lillian. Mrs. Vallish was much younger than her husband, and from the beginning determined to get him out of the coal mines. She convinced him to let her open a small grocery store catering to miners' families. The store prospered and she then persuaded him to leave the mines and help her in the store. Soon she felt there was not enough profit in groceries, and, against her husband's wishes, she went to a local bank and borrowed the money to start a furniture store. Her husband refused to have any part of the new business at first, but insisted on keeping the grocery store even though it was by now barely making a profit.

As the furniture store continued to prosper, Mrs. Vallish bought a four-storied brick building in the heart of Mount Carmel. The fourth floor was turned into an apartment for the family and the other three floors were used to display the furniture.

As she continued to prosper she became interested in buying stocks. One day she gave her husband a check for twenty-five thousand dollars to go to the bank to buy a certain stock. When he got there he discussed his purchase with the president of the bank, who convinced him to invest instead in a railroad stock. Without consulting his wife, he did. The stock failed and all the money was lost.

When I married into the family some fifteen years later, the loss of the money was often the subject of quarrels between the two of them.

Lillian told me that when she was a girl the quarreling was incessant and often violent. Often, after one of the more extreme and bitter arguments, her mother would take Lillian to the first floor and leave her father in the store apartment. Her mother would begin to worry that her father, who kept a gun, might, in his despair, harm himself and she would send the six-year-old Lillian up to the fourth floor to see that he was all right.

Mrs. Vallish was ambitious for her girls, and by the time Polly had finished high school there was money to send her off to college. She didn't like it and left after a year. Dorothy, who graduated next, was sent to the University of Pennsylvania. Rita and Lillian were sent as young children to a Catholic boarding school. Rita, three years older than Lillian, flourished there, but Lillian was so homesick she became ill and had to be sent back to her parents. Rita returned to Mount Carmel for high school, where she graduated. Her mother then chose a Catholic college in New Jersey for her and went with her to register. Rita took an immediate dislike to the school and begged her mother not to make her stay. She had been told by her high school English teacher of Radcliffe College and implored her mother to send her there. Mrs. Vallish finally agreed and together they drove to Radcliffe and found there was still a vacancy for the present semester. Rita was enrolled.

When Lillian graduated from high school she first asked to go the University of Pennsylvania, but didn't like it and transferred to Radcliffe.

Rita, in the meantime, married George Mayberry, an assistant professor at Harvard and had a child. The war in Europe was in full force and students at Radcliffe were encouraged to accelerate, which Lillian did, going to school every summer except for the last one.

Rita and George now had two children, and had moved to New York City where George was book editor for *The New Republic*. They lived on Seventy-sixth Street in a large old-fashioned apartment, handsomely furnished by Mrs. Vallish. Soon after Lillian and I began going together she took me to meet them. Rita looked nothing like Lillian, taller, with dark hair and large expressive eyes—blue, as I remember. George Mayberry, much in love with his young wife, wore glasses, which gave him an owlish look. He was not handsome, but pleasant looking and always kind to Lillian and in turn to me. They had the two of us over often to their apartment for dinner before Lillian left for college, and afterward they invited me regularly on weekends for dinner or a party.

The talk at the parties of my dance friends was usually about dance and dancers: what Martha was up to, or Doris, or Charles, and the talk of my theater friends about the current plays, or the plays about to begin rehearsals, or gossip about actors or actresses.

At George and Rita's parties the guests were editors, publishers, critics, painters, and writers. I met there Robert Motherwell, just beginning to be known as a painter, and we became friends. Also Frank Taylor and his fellow editor at Reynal-Hitchcock, Albert Erskine, who had been married to Katherine Anne Porter; Richard Watts, the drama critic for the *New York Post;* Malcolm Cowley; Agnes Smedley, the war correspondent; and many others. They knew all the current writers and had strong opinions about literature. They seemed to have read everything from the beginning of time and I felt woefully ignorant. None of them except Richard Watts seemed at all interested in the theater, and indeed several of them said they found the theater boring and much preferred films. I remember Albert Erskine one evening saying he despised Martha Graham and all modern dance, that it was ugly and he much preferred ballet. Marianne

Moore was just becoming known then and I believe Frank Taylor was her publisher. Taylor was full of stories about Moore's eccentricities and everyone agreed she was a great poet. George Mayberry had just reviewed for the *The New Republic* a first novel by Saul Bellow and he was full of praises for the novel and its author. He was contemptuous of Thomas Wolfe, and was critical of my friend James T. Farrell. He thought he was well meaning, but wrote clumsily.

I had been for so long absorbed in my own writing (which none of them had ever heard of), the theater and dance, that I had neglected my reading. I began to read once again: Evelyn Waugh, William Faulkner, Katherine Anne Porter, e.e. cummings (he was a friend, too, of Agnes de Mille and she took me one day to Patchen Place to have tea with him and his wife), Djuna Barnes, T. S. Elliot, W. H. Auden, Christopher Isherwood, William Carlos Williams, Marianne Moore, André Gide, Wallace Stevens, Ezra Pound, Gertrude Stein, James Joyce, and Eudora Welty.

From my reading, it was the *Cantos* of Ezra Pound, Eliot's *The Waste Land* and *Four Quartets* and Katherine Anne Porter's *Pale Horse, Pale Rider* that I kept coming back to. Yeats, too, and, later on, Flannery O'Connor, Randall Jarrell, particularly his *The Player Piano* and *The Lost World,* and much later, Elizabeth Bishop and Reynolds Price.

I first heard of Charles Ives not at George and Rita's, because music was never discussed there, but I suppose rather at Valerie and Bernardo's. Most of the discussions there were about dance, but music was sometimes talked about. I heard of Villa-Lobos there for the first time and heard some of his music, and after

Gustav Mahler's widow Alma left after a visit, Bernardo talked on and on about Mahler's music. Then, too, John Cage did one of his early pieces for a prepared piano for Valerie, which she used for an early dance solo called *And the Earth Shall Bear It.* Through the years, whenever I was with the Segalls, there was talk of the latest Cage experiments. Often in the afternoon or early morning, before starting work at the bookstore, I would go to their apartment. Bernardo would be practicing, as he did most every day, four or five hours, and I would listen as he went over and over the pieces that he planned to play at his next Carnegie Hall recital. The music of Charles Ives became almost an obsession for me in later years. I bought all of his available recordings and read all I could about his life.

When the war ended, most of the members of the American Actors Company that had been in the service returned to New York, but Mary Hunter was now involved with the American Theater Wing, helping to start classes in acting, directing, and playwrighting for returning veterans. There was no talk of ever now reviving the company.

Bernardo Segall was teaching piano once a week at the King Smith School in Washington. It had been a very exclusive finishing school for girls from the South, but during the war years it had changed, and was now a genteel boardinghouse for women working in Washington, mostly for the government. At night they offered classes in piano, painting, and literature for the women (almost all young) living at the house. With the creation of the GI Bill, they hoped to have a full-time school with day as well as night classes. They were eager to add dance and theater to the curriculum and asked Valerie to teach dance. She talked to them of her plans for a dance theater and they were encouraging and said if she would come to Washington they would help her find performance space. She asked if Lillian and I would go with her. She said she felt this was a chance for us to do the kind of theater work we had been hoping to do. My wife and I were both intrigued with the idea, but I was fearful that with all the teaching and producing I would have little time for writing. A friend, Vincent Donehue, had just gotten out of the army and was at loose ends. I approached him about going to Washington and sharing the responsibility of starting a school and theater and he was interested. The three of us left within a month. Valerie and Bernardo were to follow later. That never happened. They came down the first year once a week, and then recitals in New York and appearances in Broadway musicals kept them away.

Lillian, Vincent, and I stayed in Washington for five years. We established an acting company, and Mary Hunter came down and directed a stunning production of Sartre's *No Exit*. Patricia Coates directed Gertrude Stein's *Yes Is for a Very Young Man*. Vincent directed Sarayon's *My Heart's in the Highlands,* and I directed Tennessee's *The Purification,* Lorca's *If Five Years Pass,* and Ibsen's *Hedda Gabler.* I wrote and directed *Themes and Variations, The Return, Homecoming,* and *Good-bye to Richmond.* Vincent directed my play *People in the Show,* with a young Eli Wallach and Jean Stapleton.

Good-bye to Richmond had a score written by Gerald Cook and choreography by Angela Kennedy, a former member of Martha Graham's company. *Themes and Variations* had a score by Robert

Evett and again choreography by Angela Kennedy, and *The Return,* a score by Robert Evett.

Washington theaters were segregated in those days, but from the beginning our school and theater were not.

My wife was the administrator for the school and along with Vincent and myself a manager of the theater. She was twenty when we married, twenty-one when we moved to Washington. She'd had no experience in administering a school or a theater, but she was from the first successful in doing both. I looked to her increasingly while in Washington, indeed during the forty-eight years of our marriage, for her criticism during the writing of my plays and their productions. Much later she was co-producer of my films *1918, On Valentine's Day,* and *Courtship.*

I was working long hours teaching, directing, and trying to get some writing done, when one day it came to me: as grateful as I was for the opportunity I had been given to have my own theater and to experiment as much as I pleased, I wanted to go back to my earlier way of writing. I felt I was a storyteller, and that I wanted to write plays simply and directly. And I thought of Trepliov's speech in the last scene of *The Sea Gull:*

"I'm coming more and more to the conclusion that it's a matter not of old forms and not of new forms, but that a man writes, not thinking at all of what form to choose, writes because it comes pouring out from his soul."

I told my wife and Vincent that I felt it was time to say good-bye to Washington and they agreed. When my wife and I returned to New York in the fall, there had been many changes in the theater and among my friends. Louis Horst was dead. Doris Humphrey was crippled by arthritis and could no longer dance and seldom choreographed. Valerie Bettis was dancing and starring in a Broadway musical with the great Beatrice Lillie. Martha Graham had expanded her company to include men and was at the height of her creative power.

I had written *The Chase* and Herman Shumlin, the producer and director of *The Children's Hour* and *The Little Foxes,* had taken an option on it. While waiting for that production to happen (it never did), Mary Hunter gave me a job teaching playwrighting and acting to singers and dancers at the American Theater Wing.

Two years later *The Chase* finally reached Broadway, but now produced and directed by José Ferrer. It was followed the next year by *The Trip to Bountiful* with Lillian Gish and Jo Van Fleet and the following year by *The Traveling Lady,* produced by Roger Stevens for the Playwrights Company and starring Kim Stanley.

Broadway, however, was beginning its slow decline, and playwrights had to look to off-Broadway and the regional theater more and more for their productions. Live television was beginning and I was hired by Fred Coe, producer of the Goodyear and Philco television series to write nine one-hour television plays. Television in those very early days had to be performed live, which meant it went out over the airways unedited, and once the performance began it couldn't be stopped. In its immediacy it was much like live theater and, among the writers working with Coe, there were two schools of thought about television's development. Some thought it should go in the direction of film and others in the direction of theater. I agreed with the latter and, indeed, the plays I wrote for television were really one-act plays, and now some forty years later they're still being done as plays. I was asked to do the film adaptation of Harper Lee's novel *To Kill a Mockingbird.* It was a success and I was offered many films after that. In all I have done thirteen. *Tender Mercies* is the only one I wrote directly for the screen. The others were nearly all adaptations of my plays except for *Tomorrow,* which I adapted from a story by William Faulkner, and *Of Mice and Men,* adapted from John Steinbeck's novel for one of the studios. All the time I was writing plays, though, which I continue to do. I have written over sixty by now, and most of them are set in the Texas town I began writing about all those years ago.

Photo Credits and Permissions

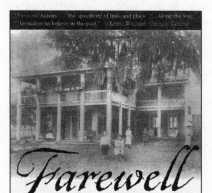